A World of Children's Games

Edited by Mary Duckert
Illustrated by Gloria Ortiz

Friendship Press
New York

Copyright © 1993 by Friendship Press
Editorial Offices:
475 Riverside Drive, New York, NY 10115
Distribution Offices:
P.O. Box 37844, Cincinnati, OH 45222-0844

Manufactured in the United States of America
Printed on recycled paper

Library of Congress Cataloging-in-Publication Data

A World of children's games / edited by Mary Duckert; illustrated by
    Gloria Ortiz.
        p. cm.
    Includes index.
    ISBN 0-377-00261-5
    1. Games.   I. Duckert, Mary.
GV1203.W836   1993
790.1'922--dc20

93-19619
CIP

To the Tibetan boys and girls now living in the Indian Himalayas, who played ball with a stick and a stone until someone from Austria sent them a baseball from America

Contents

▲ for those who cannot run
■ for all ages

Preface

Games, like legends, belong to the people. In North America, collectors of games range from J.H. Bancroft's *Games for the Playground, Home, School, and Gymnasium* (1909) to Jack Maguire's *Hopscotch, Hangman, Hot Potato, and Ha, Ha, Ha,* (1990). There are also collectors of children's games in other parts of the world. In Britain, Iona and Peter Opie did copious first-hand research on games that children 6 to 12 played out of doors without adult supervision. Alan Armstrong got to know descendants of the original New Zealanders and wrote *Maori Games and Hakas* (1973).

A considerable body of literature still exists in libraries, most of it out of print, with instructions for categories of games—girls' games, boys' games, fun for the whole family, and what to do at camp. After 1970 that kind of book was seldom published, and the few that were did not enjoy wide circulation. The emphasis has changed to the origin of games, the people who first played them, and how they were transported from one region of the world to another.

Historians and social anthropologists have sought to learn about ancient societies from the games adults and children played. That literature ranges from Philippe Ariès's *Centuries of Childhood: A Social History of Family Life* (1962) to R.C. Bell's *Board and Table Games from Many Civilizations* (1969). *The Study of Games* by Elliot Avedon and Brian Sutton-Smith (1979) is a scholarly description of games as they were played and are played today. Sutton-Smith also did research on children's games in New Zealand. Though nothing specific from Frederic Gruenfield's *Games of the World* (1988), written for UNICEF, appears in this book, this compiler used it again and again to verify accounts from individuals of the origins of games around the world.

Nina Millen broke ground in a different way in *Children's Games from Many Lands* (1950, 1965). She was in touch with mission personnel from many areas of the world and collected games that children played. The games may have been taken from Scotland, Germany, and Canada to Japan, India, and Brazil by missionaries. No matter; they have become part of the language and lore of the parents and children living there now. The games in this book that come from Millen's work are found in no other collection of games from their respective countries, although games of a similar nature are played in other parts of the world.

Most of the games in this book are described in two or more collections. The exceptions are a few, not all, of the games received from the author's reporters. The reporters began as a crew of seven children, ages 7 to 12, one in each geographic area. They were joined by adults, young people, and other children who heard about this book. There is no way to list those many people beyond the initial crew—John, Rachel, Ranee, Aziz, Betsy, Zaia, and Bonnie. It is the information from players that gives a book of games credibility. This compiler is most grateful for their contributions.

Introduction

The games in this book are intended for the enjoyment of children from 5 to 12 and their adult and adolescent leaders. The games come from the whole planet; some are as old as recorded history, and a few are as new as a seven–year–old's imagination. They range from running and chasing games to games played with pebbles, balls, cards, or string.

The Origins of Games

The games are organized in seven somewhat arbitrary geographical-cultural regions. There is no assurance that each game originated in the area for which it is listed. We know only that it is or was played there. Similar games played in different places at different times might have originated independently in those places, or they might have been brought from somewhere else. A game might die out in one place but be carried to a new place, where it flourishes. By the year 2000, there may be more children in the United States and Canada playing African and Balkan games than in the games' countries of origin, which have been weakened by famine and war.

Who Stole the Cookies from the Cookie Jar? is identified as an African American hand-clapping game, but it is played by children of all races on playgrounds and sidewalks in the United States, and a lively first cousin of it is played by children in Wales. Moreover, archaeologists in Thebes, Egypt, have found ancient paintings on a tomb wall and on sherds of a vase showing two Egyptian girls playing a similar, intricate clapping game more than 2,000 years ago.

Mother, May I? is played essentially the same way in the United Kingdom as in parts of North America. It is also played in Israel as Abba ("father"), May I? with similar ant, camel, and mouse steps. In the 1950s Jewish immigrants from the midwest settled in Israel, where they taught the American game to their children, who taught other Israeli children.

A terra-cotta group in the British Museum, London, dated 800 B.C., shows two girls playing knucklebones, or jacks, as today's children know the game. The knucklebones, made from the legs of sheep or goats, were called astragals by the ancient Greeks and Romans, who used them sometimes for gambling games and sometimes to predict the future. Roman soldiers carried the gambling game all over the empire. But gambling with astragals is found far from Rome in such places as Polynesia, where the soldiers did not go.

When school children appropriated jacks, the game over time lost its use for gambling. Today in many places playing jacks is a game of skill providing an opportunity for achievement. "Being good at jacks" is a schoolyard compliment that may be said about someone else, or it may be said of oneself as a statement of fact without being considered bragging.

The Endurance and Adaptability of Games

Some teachers, parents, pastors, and other adults who work with children bemoan the passing of traditional children's games. They report children's consuming interest in electronic video games, which they play sometimes alone and sometimes in competition with others. In the introduction to their book *Children's Games in Street and Playground* (1969), Iona and Peter Opie remark that there is a common assumption that children have lost the ability to entertain themselves, probably because of the prevalence of organized sports and television. In 1988, however, Iona Opie, on her first trip to North America, told the *New Yorker* in an interview that the disappearance of children's games is a myth. Older children come to believe it as they outgrow the games of younger children and feel superior to them. Adults, rooted in that sense of superiority, have never outgrown the myth.

In fact, rather than discarding games, children conserve them. They adapt games continually, sometimes in imitation of a complicated adult contest of skill and speed. When left on their own, they decide together on the form the adaptation will take.

For example, in a small park in the area of the embassies in New Delhi, a group of English-speaking children, none older than 10, negotiated rules for a game with a cricket bat and a tennis ball. After some horseplay, a boy asked, "Do you know how to play baseball? I can teach you. I've seen it a million times in Houston." He walked them around what he saw as the diamond. "This will be 'first,'" he announced and put his canvas hat on the ground. From "second" to "third" and "home" the children listened to some rules, one of which changed very quickly. The first batter picked up the cricket bat as if it were a Louisville Slugger and sent the tennis ball out of the park into a manicured lawn. "Out of the park is the same as three strikes!" called a girl wearing a Toronto Blue Jays tee shirt. All agreed.

Running and chasing games are ancient, and many are related to hunting and battle. Examples in this book are Springbok Stalking from Botswana and Nomads and Settlers from Iran. Foot Polo from Afganistan and Soccer and Field Hockey in the West are games in which opposing teams chase a ball. Caputre the Flag is a warlike game played in the West. Such games have been adapted to modern times. In cities of North America, children play Cops and Robbers. The Cops chase the Robbers, who try to avoid being caught.

Old card games continue to be adapted, even when the players believe they have made them up. On a day when a blizzard kept children in a small Minnesota village at home, four 11- and 12-year-old girls—Sara, Elizabeth, Caroline, and Jill—devised a card game somewhat like Go Fish and a good bit like Authors, which they called Futures. They were inspired by a huge sheet of stiff paper that had been given to Sara's mother. They cut out 16 playing cards, 4 to each girl. On each of her cards the girl drew her face and printed one thing about herself. Elizabeth's cards, for example, read as follows:

Mother—day-care director
Father—minister
Brother—musician
Future—spy

During their first game they discovered they had too few cards. After talking with Sara's mother and visiting a housebound woman next door, who helped them, they began making cards for people in the neighborhood. By late afternoon they had 48 cards, 12 sets of 4, and played the game.

According to their rules, each of four players receives six cards and asks a question in turn. When one says, for example, "Caroline, I want all your Jills," she must have at least one Jill herself. Caroline must give up any Jills; if she has none, the player draws one card from the pile or remaining cards. If it is a Jill card, she says, "Hah-hah!" and draws again. If she wants to keep the card, she must discard one. The object of the game is to make sets of four in front of the player. The game is over when a player is out of cards.

The girls went to great pains to preserve their creation. With clear plastic tape they attached the cards to several sheets of paper and photocopied four more complete sets, showing how adaptation in game making reflects the technology of modern times.

Styles of Leadership

Children continue to adapt old games and create new ones as they amuse themselves in self-selected groups. In more structured situations where boys and girls do not know one another well, a leader can teach them new games from cultures other than their own. Children admire and tend to imitate leaders who are consistently fair. Often an adult leader hears his or her own words, enunciation, and inflection coming from a burgeoning nine-year-old leader: "The rule of this game is that as soon as a deer is touched on the back, that deer becomes the hunter's helper. David, you are the hunter's helper."

Most leaders are predominantly teachers, coaches, or negotiators, depending on their orientation. Sometimes a leader may find it helpful to borrow a little from one of the other styles. In time some young players may use all three.

The Leader as Teacher

Leaders need to know how to play the games they teach. They share the object of the game and the rules with all the players. In choosing games, they consider the children—their abilities, preferences, past performance, and skills that need sharpening. Just as teachers in classrooms involve each boy and girl in learning, leaders of games include everyone somehow. Any games in this book that are particularly appropriate for children with motor difficulties and hearing or sight impairments are designated as such in the directions. When one such child is in the group, the leader can designate at the outset how, for example, someone in a wheelchair will be involved as caller in Mother, May I? mentioned earlier. Children who do not hear well or see clearly can be involved in the Vietnamese game Biting the Carp's Tail, in which the children form a long chain and the head of the carp tries to bite its tail.

Boys and girls often need to be reminded of the rules of a game. This need not be an occasion for chiding or ridicule. *The rules belong to the game, not to the teacher.* Fair play is the object so that everyone has a good time.

The Leader as Coach

Once a game is familiar to the children, there may be aspects of it that could be improved by encouragement. For example, one version of Biting the Carp's Tail can turn into a very rough game in which smaller children tend to be dragged and tugged about in an unfair manner. The leader acting as coach may (1) speak to aggressors in the group, (2) suggest another game, or (3) divide the group and play two games.

It is the coach's responsibility to see that winning, if such is the object, does not preclude a player's treating other players with fairness. The coach needs to be supportive of both winners and losers and to suggest games that require different kinds of expertise so that the same people are not always applauded or scorned.

Philippe Ariès says in *Centuries of Childhood* (1962) that in 17th-century Europe children played alongside adults in games of chance. The concept of competition was of adult origin, and as children fell heir to adult games, the games lost much of their competitive edge. Coaches need to guard against setting adult standards of accomplishment and satisfaction in games played by children for their enjoyment. Boys and girls will continue to have fun playing games by themselves, but with sensitive teaching and coaching the number and variety of games can be greatly expanded.

The Leader as Negotiator

Negotiation is a skill and an art that introduces children to the hard business of peacemaking. The leader as negotiator plays fair with everyone and affords everyone the opportunity to play fair as well.

How do we decide which of three favorite games we will play? We draw straws, think of a number between 1 and 10, flip a coin—heads or tails, kings or crowns, ships or shields, depending on the coin of the realm.

How do we decide who is going to be first? We say,

> Innicut, minnicut, dibbity-pheeze.
> Innicut, minnicut, puff! You're out!
>   or
> One potato, two potato, three potato, four,
> Five potato, six potato, seven potato, MORE!

How do we stop a game? What do we do if someone cheats?

The leader as negotiator helps the children play a game fairly and remember the rules so that they are equipped to teach others as they grow old enough and adept enough to learn new skills and move into the wider community. The negotiator says, "Let's think this through." "Shall we change the rule?" "Shall we limit the number who can jump rope at the same time?" "Hmm. We have a tie. Shall we have a play-off or celebrate two winners?"

Several of the adaptations added to games in this book were arrived at by negotiation. All the negotiators were eight years old or older. The six- and seven-year-olds gave suggestions but were not quite ready to give up the old rules even if the rules caused them trouble. They preferred to say instead, "I don't like that game. Let's not play it."

Negotiating Techniques

Whatever one's style of leadership, some knowledge of negotiating techniques is useful. Here are ways to choose It or team captains and ways to end a game.

Ways to Choose It or Team Captains

Most children who are used to playing together have one device they consider fair in choosing leaders for a particular game. Those devices may vary from game to game. In Red Rover, where strength of arm and grip is essential and where sides are chosen, the two strongest players are often made captains so that one will be on each side. In Kick the Can it is rare that anyone volunteers to be It. That person may be chosen by chance: a player is spun around three times blindfolded and then points to someone. That person is It.

In a game like Cho-cho-chuckie, being It is fun and children will volunteer. The leader might ask, "Who had the last birthday?" Some children always use a game of Paper, Scissors, Stone or an adaptation of it to choose It. "Not It!" is a game in itself. The first player to say it holds his or her arms in a big circle for all other players to touch and say, "Not It." Counting out by a rhyme is done more by young children than by older ones, who want to get on with the game. A seven-year-old girl reporter for this book likes choosing It better than playing Duck, Duck, Goose. She and her friends say, "My mother told me to chose this one, and you are It," touching the outstretched right hand of a player on each word. They start with anyone but must go in one direction only without reversing. On "It" the die is cast and that person must serve.

Ways to End a Game

Hide and Seek games are sometimes called because of darkness or mealtime. Players can agree ahead of time that It or a leader may call them in with a rhyme. In the United Kingdom the players all seem to understand, "Ally, ally in" and "Olly, olly in," but children report various chants they have learned playing with visitors from elsewhere:

> Billy, Billy buck,
> The game's broke up.
> Come in, come in, wherever you are.
> If you don't want to play, stay where you are.

In the United States reporters from the northwest and northeast chanted,

> Olly, olly oxen free!

One reporter in the upper midwest insisted on

> Ole, Ole Olsen free.
> If you don't come now, you'll be I-T.

The same reporter warned against leaders who try to trick the players by chanting,

> Ole, Ole Olsen free.
> Don't come in or you'll be I-T.

If scoring or winning is the point of the game, players should decide before playing that the score at quitting time is final or that it will be continued in a future game. Going-home time is not the appropriate moment for negotiating.

Inclusive Games

In times past, children with disabling conditions have not been invited to play with the sharp-eyed and fleet of foot. Since today many boys and girls who are physically challenged go to school in the same rooms with others of their age, it behooves their leader to help all the children learn to play together when they can. The games in this book suitable for players who cannot run are marked with ▲. Children and leaders will find other opportunities for play depending on the particular individuals in the play group. Leaders need to remember, however, that their own modeling of inclusiveness awakens the imagination of other players about how to engage a physically challenged playmate in a game.

Some of the games are marked ■ for playing with people of all ages who wish to take part. Very young children learn to be good sports by imitating their elders. Middle-aged and elderly persons may contribute games of their youth that are unknown to the youngest generation.

A New Book of Games for Tomorrow's Leaders

Why do we need a new book of games? Children straddling the 20th and 21st centuries are citizens of a new world and a new age that was only science fiction to their grandparents. Many have already played games on a continent other than the one on which they were born. A child of seven who has never left his birthplace tells his church school teacher, "When we go to the moon, we'll have to invent new games, because they have no gravity up there. Or maybe we could invent gravity."

New days demand new ways. It is not enough in a new age to treasure games just because they come from anywhere but the place we are. It is not enough to teach children games from other cultures, assuming they will, as a result, appreciate the children who played them in those distant places. What is needed is that children learn to play games fairly under their own leadership. This book is intended to instruct adult and adolescent leaders in ways of playing games with children so that children will learn just that.

Is it not a worthy purpose for educators and advocates of children all over the world to teach and encourage the kinds of interaction in games that can be played again and again with fairness and justice? Whether on playgrounds, streets, or sandlots, we know children 5 to 12 are capable of creating an arena for fair play. As their leaders, we can sharpen their skills in negotiating difficulties and solving problems, offer decision-making opportunities, and give generous amounts of time to the development of leadership.

Will we do these things? Who knows? The lawmakers, office holders, parents, teachers, pastors, and other leaders of the 21st century may outshine today's leaders at the hard business of peacemaking, because they were playing at it many years before they were working at it.

Asia East of the Caspian

Most games from India and eastern Asia are centuries old. Many were originally played by adults and only gradually became games for children. Scholars disagree on both the precise age and origin of several Asian antecedents of table games that are well known in the West. For example, Dominoes are associated with China, as are Jackstraws. The games issuing from Dominoes are numerous and traveled west with merchants and traders. Dominoes were introduced in Italy in the 18th century; some scholars believe they came from China, but there is scant proof. The wooden and plastic game pieces used by North American children today are a far cry from the inlaid bone, ivory, and ebony sets used in adult gambling games of Dominoes in China and Korea.

Jackstraws, more commonly called Pick-up Sticks in North America, is a game whose object is to remove sticks one by one from a pile of sticks without disturbing any of the others. Museum sets of East Asian Jackstraws are of finely carved ivory and were never intended to be touched by children. By contrast the wooden or plastic sticks that come in a tubular box in Western countries today make an inexpensive game for the whole family.

Chess and Pachisi are Indian games. India lost the glory of Chess to the Middle East and to Europe, where it was carried by merchants and Crusaders in the Middle Ages, but Pachisi is the national game of India. Some of the earliest Indian boards can be seen in ancient temples carved in stone. Others are made of marble and mosaic. Travelers made a cross-shaped "board" of cloth and rolled it up around the playing pieces to fit in their luggage. Pachisi-Round Trip in this book is a modern version using a simply drawn board adapted for family use.

Tangram is a traditional Chinese puzzle that has once again soared in popularity in the West. The 7-piece version in this section is the one being sold in shops today. No one has set a limit on the number of fanciful designs that can be made with the rectilinear geometric shapes. It is claimed that hundreds or thousands are possible. There is also a 15-piece version from which artists and engineers make pictures. It includes two semicircles as well as the conventional rectilinear shapes of the smaller puzzle.

Some Asian games were intended just for children and are still played on holidays and at festivals. These are the games refugees and immigrants are bringing to North America. Many have already become favorites on school playgrounds and in parks. Biting the Carp's Tail and the Vietnamese version of Follow the Leader are examples in this book. Children from a new Korean church were asked at a picnic to teach boys and girls from an established American Presbyterian church one of their national games. They chose Shadow Tag and were most surprised when all the American children already knew it, even the trick of hiding one's shadow in the shade!

Pachisi-Round Trip ▲ ■

Players: 3 to 4, ages 8 to 12
Equipment: Pachisi board, two dice, and four counters of
    one color for each player

The traditional game of Pachisi has been played in India for more than 1,300 years, and it is still played by adults and children. Pachisi-Round Trip is a new game devised at a Hindu and Christian family gathering so that the children present would learn about Pachisi. It has been played by children across the United States since then on homemade boards. The grid may be drawn on poster board or a piece of plastic that does not resist the ink of felt pens. Counters may be shirt buttons or pennies covered with construction paper circles of yellow, green, red, and black. Two dice from any other game are needed.

Pachisi as originally played is a game of war. It has some aspects of cooperation, but this version of the game features cooperation. In both games the object is to travel from home all around the board and arrive home again. In the parent game, players keep returning home again and again as the result of being captured. In this version, players are sent on missions into neighborhood, city, nation, and world from which they can be rescued by another player and brought back to the board. They travel with four counters and try to reach home in the company of four more. When playing partners, the object is to double up with one's partner's counters and get home before the other set of partners.

Moving Around the Board

To begin, each player chooses four counters of the same color and places them in the circle to the right of the leg of the cross in front of him or her. To decide who plays first everyone rolls a die. The person with the lowest number starts by placing one counter in the home box in the center of the board and throwing the dice. The player advances the counter toward himself or herself the same number of spaces as shown on the dice. The player advances twice the number on the dice if both dice show the same number. Players follow the arrows counterclockwise around the board toward home. A player's counter

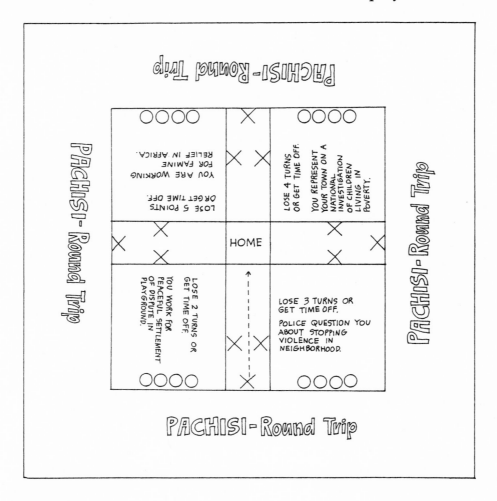

arriving at a space occupied by another player's counter is sent on a mission to the immediate right of the space, where it stays for the prescribed number of turns or until another player brings it back to the board. However, an X in the path of the counter is a safe zone. If another player's counter lands on a X spot, both can remain and continue playing.

Counters on Mission

When a counter is sent on a mission, the player to whom it belongs puts a second counter on home and begins to play it during the turns lost by the first counter. The only time for a player to begin another counter is when one is sent on a mission. All counters must start at home and return home for a player or players to win the game.

If an individual player (or a partner if playing partners) throws two dice with the same number, he or she has the choice of advancing a counter or bringing a counter on a mission back to the playing path. The retrieved counter rides on the top of a counter belonging to the rescuer for the remainder of the game. It is to the advantage of all players to bring counters back on the pathway toward home because no counter can enter home without the company of another. As soon as counters are doubled, both players to whom they belong can move them at either player's turn. The color of the counter on top determines which final path toward home the counters take.

Advancing Toward Home

Upon the counter's arriving at or near the center safe zone at the bottom of a player's final path toward home, the player must throw the exact number on the dice as needed to get home. If a counter is resting on the center safe zone, the player needs a total of nine to get home. The player may advance from there, but it is wise to stay six to eight spaces from home since there are more ways to throw these numbers than those above or below them.

Winning

In a game of four players, the partners play across from each other and double up counters as soon as they can. In a game of three, there is a total of 12 counters. The first player to get all 4 counters doubled with any 4 others on the board is a likely winner. In either game the first player or side with 4 double counters to reach home is the winner.

Somersaulting
Ultbazi

Players: any number, ages 5 to 7

Somersaulting is a village street game that is also popular with young children at family gatherings. It is fast-paced.

The object of the game is to see who can turn the greatest number of somersaults without stopping. When a large group of children play, an adult sometimes appoints two leaders to organize a relay race. The leaders choose sides and line up the players in two columns. At a given signal the first two begin somersaulting. As soon as the first player on a side stops rolling, the next one begins. Those who finish stand to the side and cheer for their teams.

Indian Hopscotch
Ikri-dukri

Players: 2 or 3, ages 8 to 12
Equipment: a piece of chalk and a fragment of a clay pot or flat stone

Ikri-dukri is a Hopscotch game played in village streets that requires endurance and skill. For other versions of Hopscotch see page 72 (South Africa), page 38 (Myanmar), and page 96 (United Kingdom).

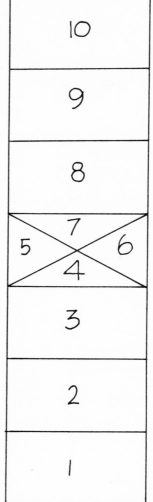

One person draws the diagram on the ground with a stick or on a sidewalk with chalk or the side of a small rock (see accompanying diagram). The object of the game is to push the *thippi* (a flat stone or a piece from a broken clay pot) with the toe of one foot as one hops on it from one numbered space to the next. When a player loses balance or misdirects the *thippi*, he or she stops and waits for another turn in which to begin again. The winner is the person who can hop on one foot from spaces 1 to 10 and kick the *thippi* at the same time.

Goli

Players: children of any age playing in small groups
Equipment: marbles

This street game is an uncomplicated game of marble shooting played best by children near the same age and of equivalent skill. Older ones teach younger ones about Goli—how to recognize one's own marbles and how to reclaim them from the hole quickly so that no one older or bigger can take them away. Traditionally played by boys in India, Goli can be enjoyed by girls as well.

The game is played on a level portion of ground. A player hollows out a small hole with the heel of one foot about six feet away from a starting line. The players take turns trying to shoot their marbles in the hole or knock other players' marbles away from the hole. The art in Goli is to do both at the same time. A game can take a long time to complete because the hole is small and it is easy to keep missing it.

Touch Wood or Die

Players: 2, equally matched at running

Forms of this Indian village game are played in many places in the world. Some scholars believe that rather than its traveling from one country to the next, the children in each area simply devised it as a kind of tag when they sought variety in their play.

Indian children play the game in twos. The chaser tries to catch the chased one to a place where he or she cannot touch wood for safety. The quarry can run from door to door or through a bazaar with its many wood-frame booths. The chaser tries to manipulate the quarry into a place where he or she is caught and becomes the chaser.

Move out of the Circle

Players: 2 teams of 4 to 10 players each, ages 8 or above

This game, described for this book by an eight-year-old boy and his mother, is popular in Bangladesh. A version of it, called Sol, is played in Guyana, which has a large south Asian population.

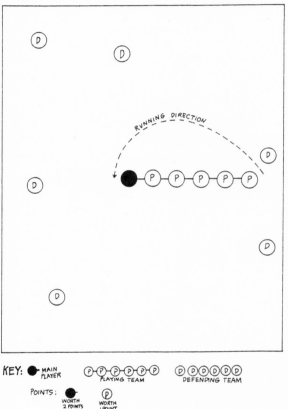

The game is played on a large, flat field. The two teams are called the playing team and the defending team. Each team has a "main player," who chooses the other members of the team. To begin, the playing team stands in a chain midway down the field stretched from the center to one edge with the main player at the end of the chain toward the center (see diagram). The defending team members take positions anywhere on the field.

The object of the game for the playing team is to reach the edge of the field without being touched by the defending team. The team members in the chain must run from the far end of the chain toward the center, run around the main player, and then dash for the edge of the field without being touched by a player of the defending team. The main player cannot leave the center until all the other team members have left the chain.

Each player reaching the edge of the field untouched scores one point. The main player reaching the edge safely scores two points. After everyone has reached the edge safely or been touched, the defending team becomes the playing team. The former playing team take positions on the field as defenders. After each team has had a turn at playing and defending, the one with the higher score is the winner.

Hiding Stones ▲

Players: at least 8, ages 5 to 8

This game is reminiscent of the North American game Button Button. It is a game with two teams and is more competitive than its Western relative.

The group divides into two teams seated in parallel columns with each player's feet touching the back of the player ahead. The person at the head of one column is given a small stone to hide under the knees of one player on his or her team. The hider takes great pains to pretend to hide it under every set of knees. The person at the head of the other team must try to guess where the stone is hidden. If the child guesses correctly, a player from the hider's team goes to the guesser's side, and the guesser becomes the hider. If the child guesses incorrectly, a player from the guesser's team goes to the hider's side. After a specified amount of time, the team with the greater number of players wins the game.

Hopscotch Squat

Players: at least 2, ages 7 to 10
Equipment: a piece of chalk or a small rock and small stones
as laggers

Hopscotch is played all over the world with a wide variety of diagrams. In Myanmar the children squat on their heels with their hands on their hips, jumping from one square to the next.

To play the game in the West, one person draws a simple hopscotch diagram (see page 96). Everyone practices jumping from a squatting position. Then the children begin to play by the usual rules, using the new jumping technique without toppling over.

Leap Frog

Players: at least 10, ages 8 to 12

Leap Frog is a lively game played by the children of Myanmar on Buddhist holidays. It is fast-moving and can be rough.

Two players who like to run are chosen to be the first runner and chaser. All other players kneel in a circle, bend over, and touch their knees, leap-frog style. The runner and chaser race around the outside of the circle. If the chaser touches the runner, the chaser becomes the runner and the runner joins the circle. The runner can leap over any child in the circle and then stop suddenly in front of a player inside the circle. That player becomes the chaser.

Biting the Carp's Tail

Players: 8 to 20, ages 7 to 12

This game, played in Vietnam, traveled to the United States with the first refugees from the Vietnam War. Because it can get rough, it is best to play it with children of about the same age, size, and strength.

Boys and girls form a line holding the waist of the person in front. The line is the carp. The object of the game is for the leader, pulling the line after him or her, to try to catch and hold the player at the tail end. The last player tries to pull the line in the opposite direction of the leader's path.

Follow the Leader

Players: 6 or more, ages 5 to 6

Young children from Vietnam played and taught this game, through their Vietnamese interpreter, to boys and girls in Pennsylvania who welcomed them as refugees.

The game begins when the adult leader chants, "This is the way the elephant goes." She or he imitates an elephant, and the boys and girls join in the chant and imitation. The leader then says, "Who wants to be leader and imitate another animal?" A volunteer takes the leader's place and the game goes on. The adult leader stops the game long enough to change leaders until the children can no longer think of animals they want to imitate.

Listen to Me

Players: at least 5, ages 5 to 8, and an adult leader
Equipment: blindfolds or paper bags to go over heads

This game is played by young children at the time of Tet, the Vietnamese New Year's celebration.

To begin, the leader blindfolds It, and the others stand about the play area wherever they choose. The leader takes It by the hand to meet each player. When It is in place again, the children clap. It tries to find each player again by using his or her ears instead of eyes. While they clap the children must stay in place. After a child is found, he or she stops clapping. The first game is over when all children have been found and touched by It. Everyone who wants to should have a chance to be It.

Eagle and Chickens

Players: 8 to 20, ages 5 to 8

There are several games similar to this one played among Chinese children. Residents of the United States who grew up in various places in China and Taiwan have taught their children the game.

The game consists of a mother hen with a brood of chickens and an eagle who wants to devour the youngest chick. To begin, the players make a line of chickens, hands on shoulders of the person ahead, with the mother hen in the lead. The eagle stands five or six feet away from the hen. Then the eagle darts toward the last player in line. The line of hen and chicks, always hanging onto the shoulders in front of them, turns and twists about, trying to confuse the eagle. When the last chick is tagged, he or she is out of the game. The game is over when all chickens are caught. No one is idle for long; the game goes fast.

Tangram ▲ ■

Players: 1 or 2 per game, ages 5 to 12
Equipment: graph paper, cardboard, scissors, sheet of colored paper

Tangram is a seven-piece puzzle in regular shapes that can make all sorts of figures. It probable began in China about 1800 as a family pastime and immediately became popular.

To make the puzzle a player transfers the accompanying diagram to graph paper. The graph paper is then pasted on a cardboard and cut apart. Then each piece is covered with colored paper, all the same color or different colors. The pieces are then assembled to represent buildings, animals, people, or abstract designs. A child can enjoy making figures alone or with another person. Older children try to duplicate or outdo the other person's Tangram.

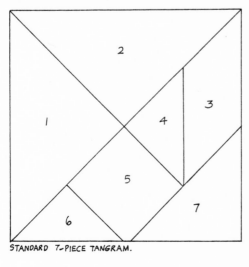

STANDARD 7-PIECE TANGRAM.

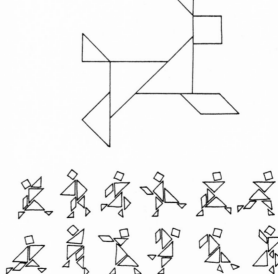

Paper, Scissors, Stone

Players: 2, ages 5 to 12

In China and Japan, children use this game to decide which team has first choice to play. The game is played almost the same way in North America, Europe, the Middle East, and Indonesia.

One person makes a fist with the right hand and pounds it on a surface, challenging the opponent, who also makes a fist. They say together, "Paper, scissors, stone." On "stone" each player makes one of three signs:

> **paper**—holds up all five fingers of the hand
> **scissors**—holds out index finger and second finger with the other fingers tucked into the palm
> **stone**—keeps the right hand in a fist

To decide who is winner in this game of chance, the players say, according to which signs they have made:

> "Paper wins over stone because it can wrap around it."
> "Scissors win over paper because they can cut it."
> "Stone wins over scissors because it can break them."

If both players make the same sign, they try again.

Shadow Tag

Players: 6 or more, ages 5 to 7

Young boys and girls play this game on sunny days in Korea. It is almost the same tag as is played in Australia as Shadows, in England as Shadow Touch, and in the United States and Canada as Shadow Tag. What is different is the age of the players and the respect for rules. In Korea a player is as good as caught should he or she "lose" a shadow by standing under a roof.

The person who is It chases a child's shadow until It steps on the shadow. Then the child whose shadow is caught becomes It.

Hiding Eyes
Me Kakushi

Players: 10 to 20, ages 5 to 8
Equipment: blindfolds or large paper bags

Girls enjoy playing this game in Japan on March 3, when they observe Girl's Festival, but it can be played by boys as well.

To begin, one child is blindfolded. All others stand in a circle around her or him. The child holds out a hand, palm up, and the circle of players walks around her or him. The child can command those in the circle to tiptoe, jump, hop, or clap. In turn, anyone in the circle can extend a hand to touch the outstretched palm. If the blindfolded person can take hold of a finger or the hand of the player, that person comes to the center, is blindfolded, too, and extends a hand. The game continues until all are blindfolded but one.

Middle East

For centuries the Middle East, which includes western Asia and northern Africa, has been a crossroads for players of games and collectors of games. Although Iran claims to have originated Hockey and Ethiopia Caroms (a kind of pocket Billiards), most old games played here by children are common to children all over the world. In modern times the in-transit areas of air terminals are places where children play, sometimes for hours, while adults surround them. Until the early 1970s, Beirut, Lebanon, had such an airport. With the onset of armed conflict in that country, Beirut lost its function of being a crossroads for young game players. Athens and Nicosia, Cyprus, became the in-transit playgrounds for globe-trotting children.

One distinguishing feature of games from countries with hot weather is that many of them are played at night, even by young children. Members of the extended families sit around watching as the children play. Many of the games involve running—tag, team games, and run-till-you-drop. An adult reporter for this book said, "It is so hot during the day that children can't run. But children *must* run sometimes, and just before they go to bed is the best time."

Another feature of the games from this region, although it is not unique to the area, is their imitation of the work of adults. Every society has games reflecting occupations of adults, but the nomadic culture that is dramatized in games is a novelty to most children of towns and villages. Down Come the

Tents from Libya and Algeria reenacts the moving with grazing animals that is a major activity of a whole nomadic community. The game is raucous fun for young children, who make believe they are the tents! The fact that urban five-year-olds can enjoy acting out such an ordeal is reason enough to encourage their playing it over and over.

In the Middle East, boys and girls often play separate games or in teams against each other. The same games or similar ones are played in Scotland, Canada, and the United States, but they are not so likely to differentiate players by sex. Some of the quiet games like Find Me from Yemen are considered traditional girls' games in the Middle East, but today in the West they are thoroughly enjoyed by young boys as well as girls.

Foot Polo

Players: 2 teams of 4 players, ages 7 to 10, and a leader
Equipment: hockey sticks and a paper bag stuffed with
    crumpled newspaper and tied shut

Foot Polo is an outdoor game played by children in many countries of the world. In Afghanistan, Iran, and Turkey it is played particularly by boys, imitating men, who also play the game. In the United Kingdom, United States, and Canada, a similar game, Field Hockey, is played by girls.

    The leader chooses two captains and they or the leader forms teams with three other players on each side. Everyone needs a hockey stick. One person marks off goal lines at each end of the playing field. The object of the game is for each team to push the paper-bag ball with their sticks along the ground toward the other team's goal line in order to cross it and thus make a goal.

    To begin, the captains face each other in the middle of the field with their players standing behind them. The leader throws the ball in the air between the captains, who try to hit it with their sticks toward a team member. The ball is never touched by team members but pushed with the hockey sticks. A game of five goals is satisfactory.

Draw a Pail of Water

Players: 8 or 12, ages 5 to 8

Variations of this game are played in several parts of the world from Greece to Scotland, but among the Uzbek people of southwestern Asia, the game is part of the whole mythology that has developed around Timur (Tamerlane), a 14th-century conqueror born in that region. He provided water for people and animals in the arid country in the days before modern irrigation. Games, superstitions, and stories were made up over the centuries as people traveled back and forth along the road to Samarkand. This particular version is popular with the youngest school children.

To begin the game, four children stand in a square and join hands across diagonally to form an X. The other players stand in a circle around the four players holding hands. The four say

> Send a lady's daughter
> To draw a pail of water.
> Father's a king, Mother's a queen,
> And two little sisters dressed in green.

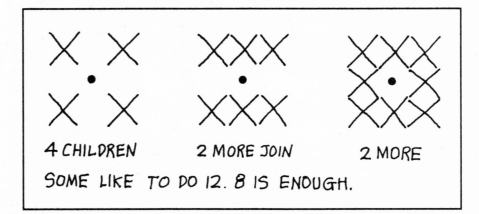

4 CHILDREN   2 MORE JOIN   2 MORE

SOME LIKE TO DO 12. 8 IS ENOUGH.

Then they raise their hands high and call the name of a child in the circle: "*(Name)*, rush in." The child runs under the arched arms and stands by two of the four players. Then they recite the verse again and call for another in the circle: "*(Name)*, rush in." After that child rushes in, the two newcomers join hands, making a formation of six. They say the verse again and call two others one at a time, and two more newcomers join the formation. The same procedure may be repeated. Eight is a manageable number, but some groups like the challenge of 12.

Pyramid ▲

Players: 2 to 4
Equipment: 7 to 9 walnuts

Pyramid is an old game played outdoors wherever walnuts are grown. It can be played with partners, and there can be a wide age range. If one player is a consistent champion, he or she can wait while the other players place or show.

The players pile up five walnuts in a pyramid. Each needs another walnut to serve as a bowling ball. Taking turns, each player tries to knock over the pyramid. Whoever succeeds gets another turn. The one who knocks it over three times in a row is the winner.

Nomads and Settlers

Players: 2 sides of 10 or more players, ages 8 to 12
Equipment: dozen or so stones or soft-drink cans

This outdoor game reflects the ancient conflict between a settled farming population and wandering herdsmen that was characteristic of the rural Middle East.

The players choose sides—nomads and settlers. The settlers collect a pile of stones or soft-drink cans and put them inside the playing area. They mark off a circle around the pile just large enough to hold their number when they form a ring facing out and hold hands to keep the nomads out. This is settlers' territory. The nomads draw another, much larger circle around the settlers' territory. This is no-man's-land, in which nomads are safe.

The object of the game is for the nomads to seize the settlers' goods without being captured and for the settlers to chase the nomads and reclaim their goods.

The nomads charge the circle of settlers by pushing through the clasped hands or ducking under them. They must not use their hands to get inside, only their heads and shoulders. Once they collect their loot, they must be permitted to leave through no-man's-land. After the raiders are outside the larger circle, the settlers can give chase and touch them with both hands on their backs. The settlers must take care to scatter, because while they are chasing one or two nomads, other nomads can enter and carry away more loot. Any nomad who is captured remains outside no-man's-land. The game is over when the settlers have no more goods to steal or when all the nomads have been caught. Older children play the game with speed and fervor.

Banosha! Bendeshesha!

Players: 2 long rows of boys and girls, ages 8 to 12

This game is somewhat like Red Rover (see page 117). Boys and girls play it on April 23, Turkey's Children's Day. In some communities, treats are free for children. The date is also Grand National Assembly Day, when the children's older sisters and brothers get elected to Parliament for a day or try to run the city halls around the country.

Two children whose birthdays are closest to April 23 are chosen as team leaders. They take turns choosing their teams, two and three players at a time. The two teams form two lines, holding hands, and stand facing each other about 20 feet apart. One is Banosha (buh-NOSH-uh). The other is Bendeshesha (BEN-duh-SHE-shuh). To begin, they cry out together, "Benosha! Bendeshesha!" The Benosha team's leader asks, "Whom do you want?" The opposite leader answers, "Send (*name*)." The requested player runs across and tries to break through at a weak link in the human chain, which resists. If he or she succeeds, the player goes back home. If the player cannot break through, he or she joins that side. Then the Bendeshesha team asks the question. The game continues for a specific number of minutes or until one side has so many players that the other concedes defeat.

What's in My Hand? ▲

Players: 4 to 5, ages 5 to 7, and a leader

A woman who takes care of young children in Lebanon played this game with her grandmother many years ago. It is a quiet game of cooperation with the leader.

The leader asks the children to imagine something small enough to fit in their fists. The first player goes to the leader and whispers, "I have _____ in my hand." The player shows a fist to the others and asks, "What's in my hand?" The others take turns asking questions, which must be answerable by yes or no: "Is it hard?" "Is it alive?" "Is it blue?" After everyone has asked one question, each one gets a guess. If no one guesses correctly, the leader says, "Here is your first clue," and puts the group on the track: "It sounds like 'dandy,'" for example, if the object is a piece of candy. If no one guesses from that clue, the leader says, "This is your second clue and you can talk over your guesses with one another." The boys and girls take turns going to whisper what they are thinking of to the leader. They tend not to care who guesses the object. The turn to ask the question is more important.

Find Me

Players: any number, ages 5 and 6

This is a game children play after the evening meal and before bedtime.

One child is It. The others hide as It counts to 10 out loud five times. It then turns around and calls out the name of one who is hiding, who answers quietly, "Find me." The player must answer It each time until It discovers the hiding place or calls another name. The players must stay in hiding until It finds them and touches them. The last one to be found is It for the next game.

Abba, May I?

Players: 5 to 10, ages, 5 or above

This street game is played in Israel and favored by girls. It is similar to Mother, May I, played in English-speaking countries (see page 95). "Abba" means "father" in Hebrew. The caller is Abba and tells the players how and how much to move in a restricted area, for example, a city sidewalk from one driveway or doorway to the next.

The players choose the caller. To the first player the caller says, "*(Name)*, you may take seven camel steps." The player must say, "Abba, may I?" and the caller responds, "You may." If the player neglects to say, "Abba, may I?" before moving, the caller says, "*(Name)*, go back to the beginning. You didn't say "Abba, may I?"

The kinds of steps the caller orders vary with the particular group of children. Here are a few:

> **ant**—The feet are spread wide apart but the steps taken are very short.
>
> **baby**—The steps are very tiny.
>
> **camel**—The steps are taken heel to toe as if one were walking on a narrow ledge.
>
> **elephant**—The body is bent over and the arms swing as the person takes large steps.
>
> **giant**—The steps are enormous but are not leaps.
>
> **pie or umbrella**—The person spins around on one foot and takes as large a step forward as possible with the other foot.

The game ends in several ways. In some games the player who reaches the finish line first gets to be the caller. The others stay in place and the former caller begins at the starting line. In other games the players, as they reach the finish line, go and hide, and the caller looks for them, or when the last player reaches the finish line, the caller becomes It for a game of Tag. The fun in the game is watching the others. Finishing first is not important.

ISRAEL

Winding Game ■

Players: at least 15, of any age, and a leader, not necessarily an adult
Equipment: recorded hora music (optional)

This game, played on a playground or in a gymnasium, is a children's version of the hora, a festive line dance for adults found in the Balkans and Israel. It can be enjoyed intergenerationally as a community activity. Children who are too short to reach the shoulders of an adult can hold hands or hang on to a belt.

The game starts with a long line of children with their arms across one another's shoulders. Following a leader at the head of the line, they wind about the play area, coiling and uncoiling. Recorded hora music helps them step, or perhaps dance, in rhythm. Sometimes the leader starts with only six or seven children and collects the others as the line moves. The game can become an endurance test, but children who tire can step out and watch for a time and then rejoin the line at the tail end whenever they wish.

Wolf! Wolf!

Players: any number, ages 5 to 7

Young children in Cairo play this game. Games similar to it are played in Europe, the United States, Canada, and Latin America.

One child is the wolf and all the others form a circle around the wolf. They chant, "Wolf! Wolf! What are you doing?" The wolf answers, "Washing clothes," Brushing my coat," Sweeping the floor," and so on. The children keep asking the question. Finally, although the players never know when to expect it, the wolf snarls, "Chasing you!" The wolf begins to chase and the others begin to run. The person who is caught first is the next wolf. Boys and girls repeat the game again and again.

A group of children in a Pennsylvania version of the game was taunting the wolf under a slide in a park. "What time is it?" they asked. "Four o'clock," the wolf answered, and the children walked away. They returned and asked again three times. At last the wolf shouted, "Time to eat you!" and charged at the group, who ran toward a flag pole. The child who was tagged by the wolf became the new one under the slide.

Rope Tug

Players: 2, ages 8 to 12, of equal strength
Equipment: sturdy rope 5 feet long and 2 balls made of
rolled-up socks

An American man working in Tripoli some years ago watched boys playing this game. It is a good spectator sport.

Each player takes an end of the rope and backs away from the other until the rope is taut. A third person places a sock ball (it will not roll easily) one long step behind each player. The object of the game is for each player to try to pull the other in the direction of his or her own ball and pick up the ball.

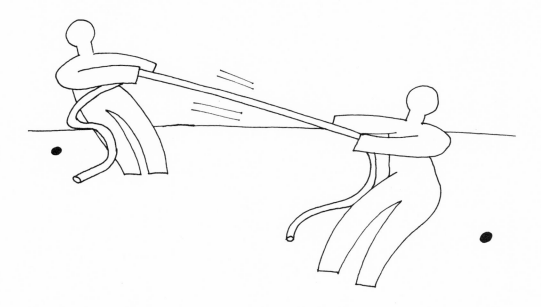

Down Come the Tents

Players: 6 to 20 girls and boys, ages 5 to 7

This game is played by young children of the Tuareg, a nomadic people, in western Libya and Algeria, in the moonlight before bedtime. Their families live in tents and raise sheep, goats, and camels. They can live in one place only so long as there is food enough for the animals. Then they must take down the tents and move.

To begin the game, boys and girls sit separately. When the adults and young people watching them clap their hands, the boys and girls join hands to make a large circle. Then they divide into small circles of three or four each. They spin around and around moving toward the center of the playing area, let go of hands, and fall to the ground exhausted. Then they are all ready to hear an adult tell a bedtime story.

Wild Horses! Wild Horses!

Players: girls ages 8 to 10 and boys ages 5 to 7

This is another moonlight game of nomadic peoples of North Africa.

The older girls mark off a race course and divide the boys into teams of two each—a horse and a jockey, who get ready to run hand-in-hand around the course three times. The girls go off and sit at a distance to watch the race. They clap their hands for the race to begin and shout:

> Wild horses! Wild horses!
> Run, run, run!

The boys get encouragement from the adults and young people watching. The winning pair bows to the cheerleaders.

Africa
South of the Sahara

Boys and girls who live south of the great desert called the Sahara represent many cultures and a great variety of experience in their daily lives. The games included here reflect that variety. They have been traditional pastimes for African children for many generations. Some games are native to Africa and are thousands of years old. Some were brought to Africa by people from other continents in the last few centuries.

Few, if any, games are played only where they were created. They have traveled with traders, explorers, conquerors, settlers, slaves, immigrants, prisoners, and missionaries. Sometimes they return to a much later generation of children, who consider them new.

In many African villages where children see few people from the outside world they play the games devised by their ancestors. Such games often imitate adult occupations such as hunting and farming, Springbok Stalking, for example, or Bringing Grain to the Storehouse.

In some African cities, such as Nairobi, Kenya, where children come from many parts of the world, they learn to play one another's games and to adapt them to their own playground or playroom. Children in South African cities play some games similar to those played in the United Kingdom and the Netherlands. These games derive from games brought by families from those European countries when they settled in Africa generations ago.

A 10-year-old boy reporting for this book from Blantyre, Malawi, was hard put to decide which game he liked better—Bawu, one of many board games, which have been played for thousands of years, or Soccer, which developed from Association Football in the late 19th century. Both began as adult games and have been adapted by children.

Bawu, which is very popular in Malawi, and Hus and Wari, similar games played in many African countries, all belong to the mancala family of board games. (*Mancala* means "movement"). Mancala games are very ancient. They were played in the Egypt of the pharaohs, as carved replicas in temples show. After the Arab conquest in the seventh century, Arabs developed variations and carried the game to other parts of Africa and southern Asia. Europeans traveling in Egypt learned the games there and took the boards home with them. Later still, African slaves took them to the West Indies.

The boards, which are used by most adult players, are of stone, clay, or fine wood and have four rows of 8 holes each. A 14-hole version of polished maple is made and sold in the United States. Children and adults in southern Africa who are too poor to buy boards scoop small holes out of the ground on which they sit.

In Africa south of the Sahara the desert grows every year. Drought and famine bring sickness to children, who no longer have the strength or desire to chase, hide, and compete in games of wit and speed. Many of them die. Others migrate with their families to cities in Africa, Europe, or Asia. Thus in Nairobi, Cape Town, Geneva, Nicosia, and Poona, boys and girls are playing the games they once played in Mogadishu, Asmara, and Khartoum.

Bringing the Grain to the Storehouse ▲

Players: 2 to 4
Equipment: 1 die and 6 shells or pebbles for each player

This is a game that boys and girls play along the Niger River. It is fun to play on any sandy beach.

Players start by building a granary in which millet is to be stored. They make a sand structure two feet square and keep it moistened. On each side they hollow out five steps starting three inches from the bottom.

The object of the game is to get all the millet (shells or pebbles) to the roof. To reach the first step, players must roll a one; they are allowed two chances to do so on the first turn only. If they are unsuccessful, they must wait their turn and try again. To reach the second step they must roll a two and so on until a six puts them on the roof. Each time they happen to roll a one they start a new shell or pebble moving up the steps.

An adaptation by an American family of four goes faster and is more fun for them. When a player lands on the same step as someone else, they proceed together and have twice as many chances with the die of getting the millet to the top. All players keep their shells on the fifth step, and all millet goes to the storehouse at the throw of a six by any player.

Jumping Game

Players: 6 or more, ages 5 to 12

This game was being played in the late 1940s when a North American missionary teacher was working with children in Liberia.

The group makes a circle with It in the middle. They all begin singing a familiar, rhythmic tune, "Rudolph, the Red-Nosed Reindeer," for example. It begins hopping from one foot to the other, extending the leg that is in the air so that the toes point downward. It then hops toward someone in the ring and extends a right or left leg toward him or her. The player in the ring must respond by pointing the proper foot toward It so that the legs do not collide. (If It extends a right leg, so must the player.) If the player makes a mistake, the toes will hit, and the two change places. If the player does not make a mistake, It jumps to another player.

Nini Nini

Players: at least 3, ages 5 to 7

Nini Nini is a foot game played by young children in Nigeria.

One child is It. The others sit on the ground in a line with their feet stretched out in front of them. It stands facing them and says,

> Nini nini kills 20,
> Nini nini kills 30,
> Nini nini kills 50.
> One was a chief,
> One was a king—
> Ogundele, the Blacksmith,
> Take in your foot.

On the last line It points to a player's foot, and the player sits on that foot. The game goes on until there is only one foot of one player left extended. The other players all pinch the foot of that player, who then becomes It for a second game.

A group of second graders in Ohio adapted the chant and action to their liking. It walks from one player to the next pointing to each foot of each player saying,

> Nini nini nini nick,
> Rini rini rini rick.
> 1, 2, 3, 4—
> Sit on this foot.

When It says "foot" and touches a player's shoe, the player does what It commands. They play until only one player has one foot extended. That person is It for another game of Nini Nini or a new game.

Star Catchers

Players: any number

This is a game that Pygmy children of Gabon play in the darkness.

One person draws two lines or sets limits 20 feet or so apart (such as from the sidewalk to the front steps). The leader chooses one third or one fourth of the players to be catchers; all others are stars. The stars stand on one or the other of the end lines. The catchers stand in between and say:

> Star light, star bright,
> How many stars are out tonight?

The stars answer, "More than you can catch!" and run to opposite sides, trying not to be caught. As soon as stars are caught, they become catchers. The last star caught becomes the first catcher for the next game and chooses assistant catchers.

Clap Ball

Players: at least 10, ages 8 to 12
Equipment: a ball made of heavy-weight socks and a stick of
    chalk

This game is played in the streets of towns and villages in Cameroon in western Africa. A mock orange (a gourd or other fruit resembling an orange) is used as a ball.

The leader divides the players into two sides of equal numbers standing about six feet apart. The leader draws a chalk line down the middle of the street parallel to the sides. Then he or she tosses the sock ball into the street. Any number of players may try to catch it, but they must not cross or step on the line. When the ball is caught, all other players clap and stamp their feet once. The catcher immediately throws the ball in the air to be caught again. Each player must remain alert in an attempt to catch the ball and to clap when someone else catches it. The faster the game goes the more fun it seems to be.

Bee Hunting

Players: 12 to 20 players, ages 5 to 8, and a leader.

This is an outdoor game of daring in which young children make fun of the dangerous activity of honey gathering carried out by adults and older boys and girls in the forests of Zaire. The children need a leader who knows the rules of the game while they are learning to play it fairly. When they are able to teach new players how to be bees and hunters, they no longer need a leader.

The leader divides the players into two straight lines of bees and hunters and sends them to opposite ends of their play area. The players in each line hang on to one another by placing their right hands on the shoulder of the player ahead.

The object of the game is for the swarm of bees to "sting" the hunters by touching them with the left hand or for the hunters to surround the bees before they get back to the hive (their end of the play area). To begin, the bees buzz and move slowly in a snakelike pattern toward the hunters. The hunters pretend to look for bees in the sky and trees, moving closer to the bees all the time. When the bees begin to touch the hunters, the hunters break rank and try to surround the bees. The bees then are free to run individually to their end of the play area. Hunters who are "stung" (touched) are out of the game. Bees who are surrounded lose their "sting." Bees who return safe to their hive and hunters who have not been stung are winners.

Antelope in the Net

Players: 1 or more, ages 5 to 8

There are chasing games related to this one played in Europe and North America in which one child pursues one other. In this African game the "antelope" is pursed by all the other children.

One child is chosen to be the antelope. All other players join hands in a circle around that player. The antelope tries to break through their clasped hands. When the antelope finally breaks free, all the other players give chase. The first one to touch the antelope is It for the next game.

South African Hopscotch

Players: 3, ages 8 to 12
Equipment: 3 small, flat stones and a piece of chalk

Hopscotch is played on every continent in many different ways. Some older children, usually girls, collect Hopscotch games, taking pride in the variations they learn from children who live in or visit other countries. This is a South African version.

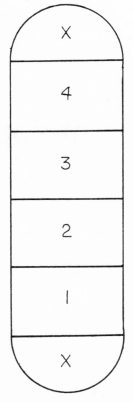

One player draws a ground plan with chalk or a stone on the sidewalk (see diagram). The players decide who will be first, second, and third. Player 1 stands in the semicircular space facing the ground plan, holding a flat stone and then placing it in the first rectangle. The player must hop into the space on one foot and with the same foot kick the stone into spaces 2, 3, and then 4 without stopping. If the player fails to hop, falls, or kicks the stone into the wrong area, he or she must wait for another turn.

When a player succeeds in kicking the stone properly, he or she shouts "Ara-uru!" on the fourth space, picks up the stone, and continues to hop back, space by space, landing with two feet on the semicircular space. Shouting, "Out-game!" the player stands with his or her back to the ground plan and throws the stone back into it. If the stone lands in one of the rectangular spaces, the player draws a circled X on the spot where it fell. After that no player can hop anywhere on the circle. If the stone lands outside the playing area, the player picks it up and waits until all other players have had a turn before having a second one.

Springbok Stalking ▲

Players: 2 at a time and many watchers
Equipment: large paper bags or blindfolds

The springbok is a fast and graceful gazelle hunted by the Bushmen of the Kalahari, a desert region in southern Africa. This ancient game makes fun of the struggle between hunter and animal.

Two players who like to run are the springbok and the hunter. All other children join hands and form a circle of watchers around them. One person covers the players' eyes with blindfolds or puts a large paper grocery bag over each head. That person spins them around several times. Everyone must try to be quiet. The watchers snap their fingers as a signal for the hunter to try to capture the springbok. When the hunter succeeds, the two players become watchers and choose two others to take their places. If after three minutes the hunter cannot touch the springbok, the game is called. The springbok remains in the circle; the hunter chooses a watcher as the next hunter and takes the watcher's place.

As few as four children can play an adaptation of the game, in which the hunter stalks the springbok around a Ping-Pong table. Watchers signal to begin and end the game.

Hus ▲ ■

Players: 2, ages 9 to 12, and a leader
Equipment: 32 shallow holes in the ground and 48 stones,
        beans, nuts, or ballbearings

Hus is a mancala game similar to Bawu, described in the introduction to this section, and a distant cousin of Wari. It is easier than Wari for children to play, once they learn the rules. Most children who play it are too poor to buy a board. The leader reads the following directions to two players. They will pick up speed quickly as they learn the rules.

    The players make four rows of 8 shallow holes in the earth. They sit opposite each other and manage the two rows closest to them. Each player has 24 pieces and puts 2 in each of 12 holes as shown in the illustration. They decide which player starts. The game is very orderly but moves very fast.

    To begin, the first player takes two pieces from any hole in his or her two rows and moves them one at a time to the next two holes to the left. If the last piece goes into an empty hole, the turn is over. If the last piece goes into a hole with other pieces, the player picks it up along with all the pieces in the

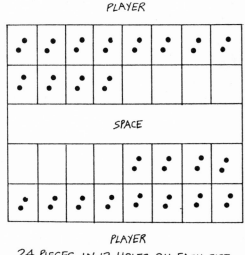

PLAYER

SPACE

PLAYER

24 PIECES IN 12 HOLES ON EACH SIDE.

hole and continues to put them in consecutive holes, one at a time.

A player must keep a sharp eye on the other person's pieces. If the active player's last piece lands in his or her front row and the other player's hole opposite it has more than one piece in it, the active player takes those pieces and puts them one by one in the holes on his or her own side, always beginning the play to the left. If the hole behind the one captured has at least two pieces in it, the active player takes those, too, and pieces from one other hole in that row. He or she puts them as usual in holes on his or her side, starting with the hole opposite the one from which he or she took the last piece. The turn is over when the player's last piece lands in an empty hole.

The player left with only one piece in each hole loses the game. In the rare event that one player seizes all the other player's pieces, it is a double win.

Children play in a series of five or seven games. If a player wins four out of five or six out of seven, the series is over. Teenagers and adults can find it challenging to play Hus with adept 9- to 12-year-olds. Boys and girls who play it often learn to react quickly. The games go fast.

Cock-a-doodle-do ▲

Players: rooster, rooster's parent, and hiders, ages 5 to 8
Equipment: a stick of chalk

This is an early morning Hide-and-Seek game from rural Ethiopia. The rooster's parent leads the game from a seated position; he or she might be someone who cannot run and hide.

One person draws a circle about six feet in diameter around the rooster's parent. The group decides who is going to be the first rooster. The rooster is It. It puts his or her head in the parent's lap while other players go and hide. After a short time It looks up to the parent and asks, "Cock-a-doodle-do?" The parent says, "No, the sun isn't up yet. Go back to sleep." It rests again, crows again, and finally the parent says, "Oh, the sun is up! Go look for the chicks."

It looks for the hiders. As soon as It spies one, they both race back to the parent's circle. If It gets there first, the hider is It for the next game. If the hider gets there first, he or she goes and hides again. The first hider to come in after It is always It for the next game. All other players are called to come in free after several have been caught.

# **E**urope

In Europe before the 20th century, children under three had their own games and toys. After their third year they played the same games as adults, sometimes with them and sometimes in imitation of them. Games that today we know only as belonging to children were played in those times by adults, Leap Frog and Blind Man's Buff, for example. Pieter Breughel's 16th-century painting of children's games shows older boys playing Leap Frog. Shakespeare mentions adults playing it in *Henry V.* A 17th-century engraving by J. Lepautre shows French peasants playing Blind Man's Buff.

When Louis XIII of France (born in 1610) was an infant, his doctor took detailed notes of his early development. At 17 months he played the fiddle and sang. At four, five, and six years he played at chess, archery, racket ball, and Prisoners' Base. The doctor does not say how well he played. All we know is that while adults were engaged in sports and games, the future king was present and taking an active part.

Carnival and other festival times especially were occasions when European children took part in the games of their elders. Pelele is an ancient Spanish game of tossing a scarecrow on a sheet or tarp. The game is associated with carnival, before Lent, but it may go back to pre-Christian times.

One of the inevitable problems arising from boys and girls playing men's and women's games was that the games fostered an early and sometimes precocious desire to gamble for money. Thomas Hughes in *Tom Brown's School Days* (1857) writes of the boys at Rugby betting on horse racing.

In the 19th century upper-class adults began to take up new pastimes. Peasants, workers, and the middle class, having less opportunity to find out about new diversions, were slow to follow their example. Children of all classes, being conservators of what they enjoy in their culture, preserved and adapted the old games, which they continue to play to this day. Prisoners' Base, played in the 14th century, has a modern cousin in Relievo and games like it in the United Kingdom. The Dreidel Game, originally a gambling game played by Jewish men in Germany, is today a favorite of Jewish children, who play it at Hanukkah for chocolates and peppermints.

When European settlers, immigrants, and refugees went to North America, South America, Africa, India, Australia, and New Zealand, they took their play and pastimes with them. As a result almost all the games that children play in Europe are known and played somewhere in the United States or Canada and in many other parts of the world.

Light My Candle

Players: 5, ages 5 to 8

This is a risk-taking game. It is known as *Aquí Hay Candela* in Puerto Rico and is similar to Kitty Wants a Corner in the mainland United States and Canada.

Four players stand at the corners of a square with It in the center. It goes to one player, extends one arm as if clutching a candle, and says, "Light my candle." "Go to another corner," the player replies. As It heads for another player, those behind Its back try to change places. It, in turn, tries to take the place of one of the shifting players. The players in the corners try to keep moving without giving It a chance to seize a corner. When It is successful, the dispossessed player becomes It. It learns to appear as if heading in one direction while at the same time being ready to pounce into another corner. The players in the corners become more and more daring as they continue to outmaneuver It.

The Peddler

Players: 6 to 12, ages 5 to 7

This is a chasing game that both boys and girls enjoy playing in the first years at school. Long ago before there were shops and stores and railroads and highways, peddlers tramped dusty country roads carrying sacks of small goods to sell to farm families. The peddler's arrival was usually an event in the isolated lives of rural people.

Players choose the first peddler by asking whose birthday is next. All other players stand in a circle holding hands with the peddler sitting in the middle. The children chant about what the peddler does and the peddler acts out the words. They begin in a sing-song manner:

> The first hour the peddler sleeps.
> The second hour the peddler sleeps.
> The third hour the peddler sleeps.

They continue through the seventh hour as the peddler goes on sleeping. Then:

> The eighth hour the peddler gets up. (The peddler stretches.)
> The ninth hour the peddler washes.
> The 10th hour the peddler eats.
> The 11th hour the peddler puts on a cloak.
> The 12th hour the peddler *RUNS!"*

At this point the children let go of one another's hands and run helter-skelter while the peddler chases and tries to catch one. The first person the peddler touches becomes the next peddler.

Old Mrs. Winter

Players: 10 to 20, ages 8 to 12, in two teams
Equipment: a head scarf

This game of chase has cousins in Switzerland and the upper Midwest in the United States. It is also called Old Lady Winter and Old Man Winter. Mrs. Winter is a head scarf.

The object of the game is for one team to keep the other team from capturing Mrs. Winter. To begin, the players form two teams—friends and catchers—by numbering off 1, 2; 1, 2. Catchers chant, "We've come to get Old Mrs. Winter." Friends run in all directions. One friend has possession of the scarf and tries to pass it to another friend, who passes it to yet another without the catchers grabbing it. When the catchers gain possession of the scarf, they too must pass it quickly among their team members so that Mrs. Winter's friends don't reclaim it. The game goes on until the players are too tired to play.

WE'VE COME TO GET OLD MRS. WINTER

Dreidel Game ▲ ■

Players: at least 2, ages 5 and above
Equipment: dreidel top, a hard surface on which to spin it, and at least 6 counters (buttons, checkers, marbles, or stones) per player

The dreidel is a four-sided top with a Hebrew letter on each side. The letters stand for "A great miracle happened here." They refer to a time in 165 B.C. when the Jews rededicated their Temple after it had been occupied by invading Syrians. The game is played especially around Hanukkah.

Although there are legends dating back to the second century B.C. about men playing dreidel games to foil their enemies, the game began among men in Germany during the Middle Ages and has been played by children in many countries for several hundred years. Small clay and plastic dreidels are available in some candy stores, but they are easy to make at home.

Drill a hole through a small wooden cube and push through it a wooden dowel four to five inches long, sharpened on one end. Practice spinning the top. When the dowel is where it should be, pull it out, put some glue in the hole, insert the dowel again, and let the glue dry. With a felt pen print the four letters on the sides of the block. It is possible to make a top out of a cardboard cosmetics or jewelry box and a short pencil, but it is more difficult to balance it for a satisfactory spin.

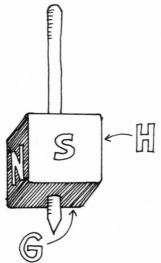

To begin, players sit on the floor or sidewalk or around a table. Each player has an equal number of counters. Every player puts two counters into the kitty in the center of the playing surface. The person whose first initial is nearest the beginning of the alphabet begins, and action proceeds clockwise thereafter. The player spins the top and does one of the following, depending on what letter faces up when the dreidel falls:

> N—Nothing. Second player begins.
> G—Player takes all.
> H—Player takes half the kitty.
> S—Player adds one to the kitty.

When a player wins half the kitty, each player adds one counter to the remainder. When a player takes all, everyone adds two to make a new kitty. The game ends when one player manages to win everything or when the players are sure they know who will win.

Ducks Fly ▲ ■

Players: 5 or more, ages 5 and above

This game is played at family gatherings or children's parties. A more complicated version of it is played in the Netherlands involving forfeits (penalties) for those who are caught, which younger children tend not to understand as being in fun.

To begin, one person, child or adult, serves as first caller. All players stay in a line or semicircle. The caller says, "All ducks fly," and because the statement is true, everyone waves arms. If the caller says, "Dogs fly," or "Houses fly," no one is supposed to wave arms. Those who wave when they shouldn't, stand next to the caller and watch the other players until they also wave their arms at the wrong time. The caller can be crafty by calling out four or five creatures that fly and quickly saying, "Boats fly," to catch players off guard. Or the caller may say, "Cats fly," and then "Catbirds fly." The game ends when there is one person left who has listened and responded correctly each time or when the group is ready to do something else.

Run, Sheep, Run

Players: at least 8, ages 5 to 12

This is a game with chasing, hiding, and informal dramatization enjoyed by people of many ages. A variation of it is played in New Zealand.

To begin, players choose a shepherd and a sheepdog. Sometimes the oldest and the youngest players get these parts. All other players are sheep. The shepherd counts the sheep by months of the year (January, February . . .) and if there are more than 12, by the days of the week as well (Monday, Tuesday . . .).

The shepherd says to the sheepdog, "I am going to market. Take care of my sheep. Don't let them out of your sight."

The sheepdog waits until the shepherd leaves and says, "I will NOT take care of the sheep. Ho-hum!" The sheepdog walks around in a circle, curls up, and goes to sleep. The sheep say, "Let's go and hide. The sheepdog is asleep." They begin to go off. No one knows when the shepherd will return.

When the shepherd comes back, he or she counts the sheep that are there: "January, March, August . . ." and goes with the sheepdog to look for the wanderers.

The shepherd and the sheepdog must tag the sheep and bring them back to the fold, count them, and discover how many more meanwhile have left. Once a sheep is back in the fold, it cannot run and hide again. Then the shepherd and the sheepdog go in search of the other sheep, who have hidden by now. When they find the sheep, they must both touch them and bring them back to the fold. The shepherd counts the sheep to see that they are all back home. The last sheep to be caught is the new shepherd. The first sheep caught is the sheepdog.

Statues

Players: 12 girls, ages 5 to 8

There are several versions of Statues played in Europe, the United States, and Canada. This one is played only by girls at school in Switzerland, but anyone could play.

To begin, players choose a shopkeeper and a buyer. The shopkeeper may be the player with the longest shoes, the buyer the one with the shortest. The buyer turns her back to the players. The shopkeeper swings the 10 other players around one by one. When she lets go of one, that girl freezes in position. When all 10 are "frozen," the shopkeeper opens the door of her shop and welcomes the buyer. The buyer taps the statues on the shoulder one by one. The statues respond by twirling, waving, hopping or jumping in place. The buyer chooses one and pays the shopkeeper. Then the buyer becomes the shopkeeper and the purchased statue is the buyer. The game continues until the players are tired of it.

Number Change

Players: 7 to 15, ages 5 to 9
Equipment: a piece of chalk

This is a chasing game to be played in a gymnasium or on an asphalt surface outside.

Players stand with plenty of space separating them. A leader draws a chalk circle around the feet of each player. The person who is first to be It walks from player to player announcing each one's number from 1 to perhaps 14.

To begin the game, It calls out two players' numbers, and those players must change circles. While they are running, It tries to stand in one of the circles first. If It fails, he or she calls out two more players' numbers and tries again. When It succeeds, the player without a circle is It for the next game. The one who is no longer It shouts, "What was your number, It?" and takes that number for his or her own. Each number belongs to a player until that player is It and loses the number. As the game goes on and many players have been It, players sometimes forget their present numbers, adding to the fun.

Blowing Bubbles ▲ ■

Players: any number, of any age
Equipment: copper wire and bubble liquid

Making soap bubbles is an outdoor game and pastime for one person or a throng. Men and women in 18th-century France developed great skill at bubble making. Toddlers can be captivated by bubbles blown by older children.

Commercial bubble liquid and wire blowers are available in variety stores and toy shops. They can also be made at home. To make the liquid, pour into a two-quart saucepan four tablespoons of glycerine and an equal amount of liquid green soap. Add one quart of water. Heat until warm, stirring occasionally. Remove from heat and let cool. Pour the solution into mustard jars or small mayonnaise jars.

To make a wire blower, take a copper wire about 12 inches long and bend it in half. Make a loop no more than 2 inches across by twisting one end of the wire to the other half and shaping the loop into a circle. Turn the other end up so that it is easy to hold without piercing one's skin.

The player dips the blower in and out of the solution until a bubble forms on the loop. He or she blows gently on the bubble and watches it enlarge and float away. Two persons playing together might see who can blow the larger bubble or send it the greater distance before it breaks. They can experiment making bubbles using drinking straws or cylindrical stirring sticks. Young children enjoy blowing through a straw into a small amount of the liquid and making a great many bubbles. More-skilled bubble blowers are able to capture one bubble at the end of the straw and slowly breathe into it until it bursts or floats away. Bubbles last longest and reflect the most colors of the prism on sunny days with very little breeze.

Prooi

Players: 8 to 12, ages 9 to 12, and a leader
Equipment: slips of paper for all players

This game is one to play at night in a gymnasium or an outdoor playground with a light switch. It is a Hide-and-Seek game with a twist.

The leader gives each player a slip of paper. On one slip only is written "Prooi" (*proe*-ee). all others are blank. The lights are turned off. The player who is Prooi hides in a roomy spot and stays there for the rest of the game. All other players grope in the dark. When they touch someone they whisper, "Prooi?" Anyone touched who is not Prooi must whisper back "Prooi," and move on. When the real Prooi is touched, he or she gives no answer at all. This is the signal for the player to stand next to Prooi and wait until the other players find them. As succeeding players approach any of the captured players, no one speaks to them but all stand together. When the leader turns on the lights, the players count their number to see if anyone has not found Prooi. Then the leader passes out the slips again for a new game.

Pelele ▲ ■

Players: 4 to 6, ages 8 to 12
Equipment: blanket and clothing and stuffing for making the
    doll

Pelele (pay-lay-lay) is the name of a game in which a stuffed, life-size doll is tossed into the air from a blanket. The doll is also called Pelele. It is an old game in Spain played during carnival time; there are varieties of it in Italy and England as well. Boys and girls sometimes make Pelele as an art project and keep him in a corner of their schoolroom long after carnival season is over.

This is a game all sorts of people can contribute to by offering clothing, assistance in sewing, and encouragement to the tossers. After the blanket toss the creators may let Pelele take up residence with a homebound child.

To make Pelele, players gather old jeans, a sweatshirt the size worn by those who toss him, men's socks, straw or many old nylon pantyhose for stuffing, a five-pound flour sack, strong nylon thread, a big sewing needle, embroidery thread or paint and brush, rug yarn, neck scarf, gloves, and a cap. Pelele has to be tightly stuffed and securely sewn in order to withstand the blanket toss.

To begin, players stuff the men's socks with straw or nylon hose. They sew the stuffed socks to the bottoms of the legs of the jeans. Then they stuff the jeans compactly with more straw or hose. Next they sew up the cuffs of the sweatshirt and stuff the sleeves. They sew the bottom of the sweatshirt to the waist of the jeans and fill the body of the sweatshirt through the neck. They fill the flour sack with more stuffing and sew it shut, leaving a generous hem to insert into the neck of the sweatshirt. Finally, they sew the sack to the neckline. When every body part is sewn solidly to another, the players can consider embellishments such as gloves, scarf, wig made of rug yarn, facial features either painted on or embroidered, a mustache, and a beret or visored cap.

It takes practice to toss Pelele. Players place the blanket on the ground with Pelele in the center of it. At least four players can hang on to the corners, but six is better. They say together, "Pelele, Pelele, GO!" On "GO!" they lift the blanket so that Pelele is tossed into the air and returns to the blanket for another go.

Call Ball

Players: 4 or more, ages 5 to 12
Equipment: any ball that bounces

This is a street game played particularly in England. It is most fun when the players have similar abilities at catching the ball and running.

The person who is It throws a ball against a wall and shouts a name of a player to catch the ball either on the fly or after it bounces once. If the player named does not catch the ball, It calls out another name. If the player catches the ball, that person is It. The game goes on for a long time if players are skillful and want to test one another's abilities.

Poison

Players: 8 to 10, ages 9 to 12

There are several playground games called Poison. This is one for older children that sometimes is fast and rough.

It or "He" (pronounced E) crosses his or her arms in front and extends fingers. Players take hold of individual fingers and chant: "What's in the bottle when the cork goes pop?" It answers any number of things ("ginger ale," "ink," "milk". . .) and then says "Poison!" The object of the game is to surprise the players. Upon hearing "Poison!" players run from It, and It chases and catches someone, who becomes It for the next game.

Mother, May I?

Players: 5 to 10, ages 5 and above

This game is similar to "Abba, May I?" from Israel (see page 56), but in England and Scotland it is played with far more intricate steps.

Children play the game in one of the ways described in "Abba, May I?" but include these steps.

baby—Bring heel of one shoe even with the middle of the other shoe.

bunny—Leap ahead as far as possible on each step with both feet held together.

banana split—Slide forward as far ahead on one foot as possible.

policeman's walk—Shut eyes and walk ahead any number of steps until It says, "Stop."

scissors—Jump forward and land with feet apart; jump forward and land with feet together.

watering can—Spit as far as possible and then stand where the spit landed.

Hopscotch

Players: 3 to 4, ages 7 to 10
Equipment: a 3-to-4-inch scrap of wood or a rock fragment
for each player to use as a potsie, and a piece of chalk

Hopscotch is played in China, Myanmar (Burma), India, South Africa, Europe, and North America. A nine-year-old English girl explained to an American friend, "Hopscotch is a *season* for us rather than a game." Her diagram is one of several used in the United Kingdom.

To begin, one player draws the diagram on the sidewalk with chalk or the edge of a rock (see drawing). The first player throws a potsie (the wood or rock fragment) into section 1, hops over the section to sections 2 and 3 on one foot, lands on two feet on 4 and 5, continues on one foot to 6 and 7, and lands on both feet on 8 and 9. The player turns around while jumping, lands again on 8 and 9 facing the grid, hops back in the same manner of coming, picks up the potsie while standing on one foot on section 2, and hops to 1 and out. Then the player throws the potsie to section 2 and waits for another turn.

The second player throws a potsie on section 1 and must jump to section 3 upon entering the game. No one can land on a section occupied by one or more potsies. A player loses the turn immediately if the potsie lands on a line or out of the section aimed at or if a player steps on a line or lands on two feet instead of one. If the first player is also first to finish, all other players have a turn before a winner is declared.

Relievo

Players: 2 teams, ages 8 to 12

This is an old Hide-and-Seek game played in northern England, Wales, and Scotland. It has many names and small local variations. The game is similar to Prisoners' Base, a more formal game played by adults as far back as the Middle Ages. It used to be played by boys alone, but today more and more often girls join the boys, occasionally playing in a team against them.

Boys and girls prefer to play the game at dusk after tea, when there are more places to hide as the sun goes down. Because the game is called when some players must go home, there is often no decisive victory.

The team leaders choose up sides and then toss a coin to decide which team will be the first hiders. A length of sidewalk or portion of ground is marked off as a den. The limits of the area allowed for hiders are announced. ("Not across the tracks, past the arch, in the park, or over Old Road.") The hiders run off to hide individually while the seekers count to 100. The seekers leave one player at the den (the den keeper) and all others go to hunt.

When a seeker finds a hider there is a bit of a ritual to follow. The seeker touches the hider on the head three times, holding on to one arm, and says, "Two, 4, 6, 8, 10—Relievo!" The seeker takes the hider to the den. The den keeper is not allowed to step inside the den with both feet. When someone from the hider's team tries to release the captive, the den keeper may catch the rescuer on the way in. But once safely in, that player touches the prisoner on the head three times and shouts "Relievo!" and they both run and hide. If the den keeper carelessly enters the den with two feet, all captives in the den may go free.

Kick the Can

Players: at least 6, ages 8 to 12
Equipment: 1 tin can

This game, though often associated with Scottish boys, is played by both girls and boys in the United Kingdom, Ireland, the United States, Canada, New Zealand, and parts of Europe. Boys, particularly as they grow older, continue playing the game with more speed and adeptness than are evidenced in these rules.

The players set prescribed limits to the extent of the hiding area and choose a goal, a place to begin at and come back to, such as a tree or a flag pole. A person may volunteer to be the first It or may be chosen for having the longest legs, shortest hair, nearest home, or whatever. To begin, a player kicks the can as far away from the goal as possible. It retrieves it, sits down at the goal, and counts from 1 to 100 while the other players are finding places to hide outdoors. It shouts at last, "Ninety-eight, 99, 100. Here I come ready or not!" When It spots someone, both run to the goal.

If It gets there first, he or she cries, "One, two, three for (name)," and the hider is caught. If the hider reaches the goal first, that player kicks the can again, runs off, and hides. This time It does not count to 100 after retrieving the can but starts immediately to look. When someone is caught and is resting at the goal, another player may steal into the goal while It is away looking for hiders. That person may kick the can and release the caught player to go and hide again.

Because it is quite possible for the same person to be It for the entire playing time, some players, particularly those 10 and under, have instituted short cuts. Some call in all hiders after three have been taken captive. Another short cut is to call the game after a captive has been released three times. The shouts to end the game vary from area to area. A common cry is "Olly, Olly, all's in free." The last person to be taken captive is always It for the next game.

Queenio

Players: at least 4, ages 5 to 8
Equipment: a medium-size bouncing ball

This ball game is played with many different rules in every corner of the United Kingdom and Republic of Ireland, usually by girls. It may be played by anyone.

To begin, Queenio (It) holds a rubber ball and has her back to the other players. She throws the ball over her head toward the playing field. When another player catches the ball, the player shouts, "Copper!" and becomes Queenio. If the ball rolls, one player retrieves it and hides it on herself. Queenio must turn around and guess who has it when the other players say, "Queenio, Queenio, who has the ball?" Queenio may make requests such as, "Sara, spin around," or "Caitlin, stretch your arms above your head." Then she guesses. If her guess is correct, she is still Queenio. Otherwise, the girl who has the ball takes her place in front and throws the ball.

America
North of the Rio Grande

Canada and the United States are heirs to a number of game-playing traditions. The oldest are those of Native Americans (Indians) and Inuit (Eskimos). These peoples were playing games in North America long before there was a United States or Canada, before there were maps of the New World, and before explorers placed flags on North American soil to claim it for their own country. Anthropologists, historians, and sociologists with an interest in these games have found that though some were played in a variety of contexts, most are remarkably the same from place to place. Allan McFarlane, author of *Book of American Indian Games* (1958), claims that a number of games were played by as many as 80 different tribes from the southeastern United States to the Northwest Coast, Plains, and Woodlands of the United States and Canada.

Children's games, played outdoors in enormous open spaces, ranged from tracking the snow (Snowy Footprints) to rolling down steep sand dunes (Roly Poly). They required very little equipment and were imitative of games and occupations of adults. The ages suggested here as appropriate to the games described are based on modern children's preferences and skills. By the time the original Native American children were 13 years old, they were regarded as adults and were no longer playing with 8- and 10-year-olds.

Later game-playing traditions are those of Europeans who

came to the New World as traders, settlers, and immigrants. Still later are those of immigrants and refugees from Asia. Each group brought its own games. In the days when rural settlements were few and far between, these games were played mostly in family settings or with neighbors. In the 19th century as houses became more numerous and more substantial but radio and television had not yet been invented, home parlor games were popular. As the volume of immigration increased and cities grew in the 20th century, recreation tended to become more specialized and move outside the home. There were street games, team sports, and games for specific age groups. Schools hired adults to teach games. Boy Scouts, Girl Scouts, Girl Guides, Boys' Brigade, and Campfire Girls were all private organizations that promoted good will through fair play in games. Churches and synagogues often maintained community centers with salaried directors of children's activities. Cities hired men and women to operate recreational programs in the parks. Since Americans do so much traveling, families even devised games to play inside automobiles.

Today, electronic games invented by commercial companies are very popular. Students of games see that trend as a falling away from communal recreation. That may indeed be an ultimate effect. For the present, all the pessimists about the future of traditional games need to do is observe hoards of school children at 8:00 A.M. waiting with adults for a parade to begin at 11:00 A.M. A specific example is the annual Rose Parade in Portland, Oregon, where miles of a city route are closed to traffic. The boys and girls come prepared to play, looking forward to an hour or two of street play and cheering when they hear on the public address system that the parade is to be delayed. At first, they play near their perches with those children they know. With the expanding crowd they welcome strangers, negotiate rules, and exchange first names. ("Hey, what's your name anyway?") What they have come there to do is play. They walk inside huge, heavy paper bags, blow and catch bubbles, using quart jars and homemade solution, draw and play Hopscotch, jump rope singly and in a group, and chase one another in Chain Tag, Pom-pom Pull Away, and Shadow Tag. (When children have water guns, diplomacy is required to keep the friendly community from panic. A teen-age boy on a skateboard, confronted by three young boys with water guns, ignored the water that struck him, took the boys to a section of the street, called for some blue chalk from the Hopscotch crowd, drew a large circle around the three, and skated away. The gunmen soaked one another.) The professional clowns engaged each year to amuse the children have very little of that to do!

Snowy Footprints

Players: at least 6, ages 8 to 12

Inuit boys and girls play this exhausting form of Follow the Leader in the snow. This is the kind of game boys and girls in cold climates can play after a snow storm has resulted in drifts of uneven depth.

The leader walks into untrodden snow, and the other players must go wherever and however he or she goes. The object of the game for the leader is to make following as difficult as possible. This is done in a variety of ways: backtracking, leaping, making the footprint especially large and slippery, twirling about so that the tracker faces backward, and running in a circle until everyone is in the circle. Then the leader turns around and tries to take the followers back to the starting point walking in the tracks they just made.

Stalkers ▲ ■

Players: 5 to 10, ages 8 to 12, and a leader
Equipment: large paper bags for blindfolds

There are many Native American stalking games of the Northwest Coast, Plains, and Woodlands, some of which are still played in wooded areas. They require that the person who is It be blindfolded. This particular game was formerly played by adults as well as children and is today an indoor as well as an outdoor game. It resembles Springbok Stalking from Botswana (see page 73).

Those in the game are stalkers, It, and a leader. The object for the stalkers is to touch It with the fingers of one hand without being detected by It. The object for It is to listen carefully for any movement of a stalker and to point in the direction of the sound, calling out, "Stop!"

In the modern version of the game, players form a big circle around It and make no noise even if the blindfolded It bumps into them. The leader quietly points to the player who is to be the first stalker. The stalker is permitted to tiptoe in stocking feet, to crawl, or to come by wheelchair but must approach It slowly so that there is time for It to say, "Stop!" If It points in the correct direction, the leader responds by saying, "Right!" and the first stalker sits down on the floor or ground. The leader then points to another player to be stalker. The stalker who manages to touch It is the next It. If no one outsmarts It, the stalker who is closest when detected becomes It. The leader is the judge of how accurately It needs to point in order to identify the sound of a stalker. Once the players have had experience being both stalkers and It, they are inclined toward fair play for everyone.

Fang ▲

Players: at least 5, ages 8 to 12, and a leader
Equipment: large paper bags or scarves for blindfolds and a
    rolled-up newspaper for a fang

Besides the imaginative games about hunting, Native American children of the Plains and Woodlands also played out their struggles with snakes, notably copperheads and rattlers.

The person chosen to be It is the snake, who is blindfolded and carries a tightly rolled newspaper to represent the fang, or means of attack. (The children traditionally tied willow branches together with long grass and covered them with buckskin.)

Players stand apart from one another at a distance of 12 to 15 feet from the snake. The object of the game is for a player to touch the snake on the head before getting hit by the fang. The leader points to the first player who is to approach It. Everyone else is very quiet as the player moves. It can use the fang only once and in one direction with each player. If the fang touches the player, he or she withdraws and the leader points at another player to advance. Any player who succeeds in touching the snake on the head is It for the next game. The leader is responsible for keeping the players from darting toward It rather than moving stealthily and for seeing that It strikes directly, not with a broad sweeping motion.

Coyote and Father

Players: 8 to 16, ages 5 to 8

Coyote is a familiar folk tale character in southwestern Indian lore. He intends to outsmart others but is not always successful. This particular game is somewhat like the Chinese game Eagle and Chickens (see page 41) and the Hawk and the Chickens from Cuba (see page 141).

To begin, players line up according to height. The two tallest players are Coyote and Father. The others are Father's children, who stand behind him hanging on to one another's shoulders. Coyote faces Father and says, "I have come to get your tallest child."

Father replies, "Oh, you can't have *(name)*. I need *(name)* to herd my sheep."

Coyote continues, "I'll take the second one then."

Father answers as before for each child in line, telling what each does for the family—tends the baby, feeds the horses, grinds the corn, rakes the hay, mends the clothing. Coyote, in exasperation, chases the smallest child at the end of the line in order to tag the child, who is then out of the game. Father and all the others twist and turn the line to evade Coyote. Each child becomes last in line and is tagged by Coyote until only Father is left. Then Coyote must catch him. As soon as Father is tagged, he turns and chases Coyote. The game is over when Coyote is caught. The smallest child may select the next game to be played.

Guessing Games ▲ ■

Players: 2 to 5, ages 5 to 12

The very same guessing games played by Native American children are played by other children around the world. They are products of the human mind in societies where mass-produced toys, commercial games, and athletic equipment are not available to boys and girls. Here are three games that can be played by and with adults as well as other children.

Stone Mountain (Stone Hill) (Stone School). As few as four players can make this game an enjoyable one. All but one person are seated next to one another on a hillside or flight of stairs. That person, who can be a child or an adult who cannot climb the hill or steps, holds a small stone. He or she puts both hands and the stone behind his or her back, approaches the seated players from left to right, shows both fists, and says, "Touch the hand where I hold the stone." When players guess correctly, they advance up the slope or staircase. When they are wrong, they stay in place. The person who reaches the top of the hill or stairs first is the next person to hold the stone. Boys and girls can play this game on a staircase as proxies for elderly people, who watch and cheer them on from the bottom of the stairs.

Pebble Guess. Two persons play this game. A young child can play it well with an elderly man or woman who enjoys guessing games. Each player has a small pebble. One player begins by moving it from one hand to the other in front of the other player, humming a monotonous tune all the while. Then with both hands in fists the player asks, "In which hand do I have the pebble?" If the other player guesses correctly, he or she gets to hide the pebble. As the game progresses it picks up speed. There is very little conversation, and a steady humming proceeds from the person concealing the pebble.

Find the Ball. This game requires a marble or small rubber ball and a blanket or beach towel. The person who is It hides the marble or ball under one corner of the blanket or beach towel while other players are watching. It tries in many ways to confuse those watching by making them think the ball is at one corner while it is still to be hidden. It may pretend to lose the ball at corner 2, and pick it up and put it at corner 3 or 4, while all the time the ball is tucked under corner 1. All the players talk together and decide under which corner It hid the ball and present It with one answer. If they are correct, It becomes a guesser and one of the guessers is the hider. If the group guesses incorrectly, It hides the ball again.

Roly Poly

Players: 2, of about the same age, and a leader

Games involving rolling down a hill are so common that there is not even one name for the category, which includes relays, races, or tests of who can roll the straightest or farthest.

A leader is necessary for Roly Poly. The object of the game is for two persons to roll down a gentle slope beginning at the same time and at the same level. They should be at least five yards apart. The leader gives the starting signal and determines who has rolled the greater distance. Generally, the pair decides ahead of time to roll three, five, or seven times. If one player wins two of three, three of five, or four of seven, the game is over.

Tanuary

Players: 10 to 20, ages 9 to 12

This is one of several similar running games played by older children at school and on city playgrounds.

The playing area is flat and about 9 or 10 yards long with a safety zone on each side. The person considered by the players to be the best runner is the first to be It. The other players line up all along the edge of one safety zone facing It, who stands halfway between the safety zones. The object of the game for the players is to run from one safety zone to the other without being tagged by It. It tries to catch as many players as possible early on so that they can help It catch the others.

To begin, It faces the line of players, who must leave one safety zone quickly to try to reach the opposite one. If three or four go at the same time, they have a better chance of evading pursuit than if they leave one by one. Eventually all must run out on the field. If all the players do not run, It stands on the field and chants:

> Tanuary, Tanuary, one, two, three,
> If you don't run now,
> I'll catch you where you be.

Each player who is tagged by It serves It by intercepting players and holding them until It can tag them.

After players successfully reach the opposite safety zone, they must immediately get ready to run back. It and the assistants chant the Tanuary rhyme to reluctant runners. The game is most exciting when players are running in both directions and It is trying to mobilize enough helpers to intercept them. The last player to be tagged is It for the next game.

Pass the Broom

Players: at least 10, ages 5 to 8 or 9 to 12, and a leader
Equipment: a common household broom and cassette tapes
and player or a whistle

This old Canadian game has several versions. Three are given.

Young Children. Young children form a circle facing the center. They put one hand on a hip and leave one hand free to grasp the broom handle when a neighbor passes it along. A player may choose which hand to use in the game but cannot change hands once the game has begun. The leader explains that as soon as the music begins, the person with the broom passes it to the nearest neighbor around the circle until the leader turns off the tape player. The person who has the broom when the music stops must hand it to the next person and drop out of the game. Each time the music stops, another person drops out. The winner is the one who is left holding the broom all alone.

Ages 9 to 12. When the players are 9 to 12, easily 20 of them can take part. Instead of taped music a whistle is the signal to begin and to stop passing the broom. The broom can be passed in either direction by any player. When the leader blows the whistle to stop, the player with the broom gives it to any player in the circle and goes to stand inside the circle. As the game goes on, those who are still passing the broom are fewer and fewer but must keep their original places, running to the next player with the broom and running back home. The leader determines both the speed and the suspense of the game by

varying the length of time between whistles. The last person left in the game can hold the broom for the next game or choose a new game instead.

Norwegian Airport Version. This version was created in a Norwegian airport by Canadian children waiting for delayed flights to Canada when more than half of them suddenly left on a jet airplane. Players are from 5 to 12 years old. At the sound of the whistle the broom is passed in one direction only. Players keep one arm behind their back and one arm in front to pass the broom. If a player and the player's neighbor both have their hands on the broomstick when the whistle is heard, they are safe and remain in the game. The broom must be in one player's hand when the whistle is blown for that person to be out of the game. As players drop out and watch the game, the circle gets smaller and smaller. The game ends when there is only one person left.

Treasure Hunt ▲ ■

Players: 10 to 20, ages 8 to 12
Equipment: an object to hide and a piece of chalk or stick

There are several games of looking for a hidden treasure that older children find challenging. This one involves following a map drawn on the ground.

The object of the game is for one team to find a treasure within a specified area—a park or playground—that the other team has hidden in plain sight and that is accessible. The treasure might be a small box, metal coaster, sardine can, or yo-yo.

The team that hides the treasure draws a map on a sidewalk with chalk or in the dirt with a stick. The seeking team can come back and look at the map at any time. A period of time—two minutes, perhaps—is given to find the treasure. After the time has elapsed, rather than concede defeat, the seeking team may ask a location question. Experienced players usually ask in which quarter of the territory the treasure is hidden. If they do not find it in the specified amount of overtime, the hiding team takes the seeking team to the treasure and the hiding team gets to hide the treasure again. When seekers find the treasure they are the next ones to hide it.

Complicated variations of Treasure Hunt are played in the context of family, school, or religious or civic group. Generally, the map is printed but can refer to any park or playground. Additional clues are printed in the local newspaper or group bulletin. The treasure may also be a mystery hinted at in clues but always in plain sight and accessible to a passerby. Though there are often prizes, most victorious teams report that the pleasure is in the game, not the reward.

Squat Tag

Players: at least 3, of well-matched running skills

The many versions of Squat Tag played around North America have similar rules and continue to take on new names for the old game.

In all games one player is It and chases the other players until one is tagged and then becomes the new It. When a person being chased squats, that player cannot be tagged. Most games specify three squats per player. When there are only three or four playing, it is easy to keep track of the number of squats. In a large group, it is more efficient, and results in fewer arguments, to suspend that rule. Some of the variations follow:

Animal Squat. The player squats and calls out the name of an animal.

Cabbage Squat or Squashed Tomatoes. The player squats and calls out "Cabbage!" or "Squashed tomatoes!"

Pardon Me. The squatter must give a new excuse at each squat—"I turned my ankle," "My foot itches," and so on.

Three Bob and Run for Your Life. The squatter gets only three squats but can stay in the game after that until tagged by It.

Chain Tag
Link Tag

Players: at least 5, ages 9 to 12

This game is played on school playgrounds in England and Australia as well as in Canada and the United States. It can be very rough, and a player who cannot keep up with the fastest runners should be encouraged to watch. It is best played by older boys and girls of near-equal running ability and physical stamina.

The object of the game is for It to catch all the players. To begin, It pursues a player until he or she is tagged. The two clasp hands and It pursues another player, who, upon being tagged, takes the first player's hand and runs along as It pursues another player until all are caught.

Red Rover

Players: at least 10, ages 5 to 7 or 8 to 12

Red Rover and games like it are played in Australia, New Zealand, and the United Kingdom as well as Canada and the United States. It is similar to the Turkish game Banosha! Bendeshesha! (see page 53).

To begin, the players divide into two teams by counting off: 1, 2; 1, 2; 1, 2—leaving to chance the physical strength of each team. The two teams face each other from two lines 10 yards apart. The left end player of one team calls out to the other team,

> Red Rover, Red Rover,
> Let *(name)* come over.

The members of the calling team grasp hands tightly. The runner from the other team looks for a weak link between players and tries to break through the line. If the runner is successful, he or she chooses any player from the calling team to join the other team. The runner who cannot break through must join the calling team. The game may go on until a team is so weak it surrenders or until the players are ready for another game.

Stoopball

Players: 1 or 2, ages 8 to 12
Equipment: a hard rubber ball that bounces well

There are several city ball games and many neighborhood variations by this name. In New York City the ball that is used has come to be called a spaldeen, probably named after A.G. Spalding, a manufacturer of sports and athletic equipment.

The simplest way to play is for one person to stand about four feet away from a set of steps. The player throws the ball at the steps and tries to catch it on the first bounce. If the ball hits the riser of the step, bounces back, and is caught, the player gets 1 point. If the ball hits the outside edge of the step, bounces back, and is caught, the player gets 10 points. If a person misses a catch, the score is minus 1. A lone player might decide to play to 100 points.

When two are playing, one is a fielder and catches the ball that the other pitches at the steps. Scoring is as above with the fielder earning the points. The pitcher gets three outs—balls that bounce in other ways than those described—and then changes places with the fielder.

Float Tag

Players: 3 or 4, ages 9 to 12

This is a city game of tag first played by older teenagers and then adapted by younger boys and girls who had watched it. The game is seldom played by more than four players and generally for a short period of time.

One person, It, is challenged by the others to chase them around a city park or recreational area. Those being chased climb on monuments, stone walls, ledges, in trees, and on play equipment. They try to leap from one resting place to another. To catch a player, It must touch him or her while that person is in the air or at a rest after a rapid count of "1, 2, 3 for *(name)*."

Stickball
Peggy

Players: 2 to 4 or 6 depending on the rules
Equipment: a broomstick or bat and a softball or tennis ball

Ball games played in the city street or in small vacant lots probably began as a variation of softball. In some games, boys and girls play in teams and have four bases. In other games they use one base only. Those players who use a softball pitch the ball underhand to the batter. Those who use a tennis ball or hard rubber ball bounce the ball to the batter.

A game between two people goes like this: The pitcher throws or bounces the ball to the batter. If the batter hits the ball, he or she runs from home plate to the base and back, a distance the same as from home plate to the pitcher's mound. The pitcher runs after the ball and tries to tag the batter between the base and home. If the pitcher catches the ball on a fly, the batter is out. The batter is allowed three strikes or four foul balls before going out. Then the batter and pitcher change places.

With four people playing there is a pitcher and a fielder on one team and a batter and a catcher on the other. When the person at bat is out from being tagged on a run, having three strikes or four fouls, or having a fly ball caught, the catcher is the next batter. The team retires to the field after the second player's turn at bat.

Boys and girls of eight and older who play Peggy at school often use a real bat and softball. They may have more than one base, but often they do not. Rather than choosing teams, they play "work up" with six people. Each time there is an out everyone moves closer to becoming a batter. The order is from center fielder to right fielder, to left fielder, pitcher, catcher, and batter. Experienced batters know how to hit ground balls to areas that are away from fielders and to bunt a very short ball away from the base so that the pitcher has to come forward to pick it up.

Children in kindergarten and early elementary grades enjoy playing Peggy, especially when one older boy or girl acts as coach. Because the younger ones are not capable pitchers, the distance between the pitcher's mound and home may need to be shortened. An elaborate form of this game, which probably arose independent of it, is The Churches (see page 126).

Who Stole the Cookies from the Cookie Jar?

Players: 2, ages 6 to 8

This street game is a clapping game similar to the one archaeologists found pictured on a wall of a centuries-old tomb and a vase in Egypt. African American children claim it as theirs, but it is popular with many other children as well. Younger children learn it by watching older children.

Two children face each other and begin a clapping rhythm with (1) hands on knees, (2) hands clapped together, (3) right hand to partner's right hand. (4) left hand to partner's left hand, (5) both hands to partner's hands. Then one child begins to chant a line in rhythm and the other answers as they both clap in the ways listed above.

1	2	3	2	4 2	5
Who	stole	the cookies	from the	cookie	jar?

1	2	3	2	4 2	5
Who	stole	the cookies	from the	cookie	jar?

2	1	2	3	2	4 2	5
Who,	me	stole	the cookies	from the	cookie	jar?

2	1	2	3	2	4 2	5
Yes,	you	stole	the cookies	from the	cookie	jar?

2	1	2	3	2	4 2	5
Not	I	stole	the cookies	from the	cookie	jar?

2	1	2	3	2	4 2	5
Then	who	stole	the cookies	from the	cookie	jar?

Hiram and Mirandy ■

Players: at least 12, ages 5 to 12
Equipment: paper bags or scarves for blindfolds

Collectors of games have found Hiram and Mirandy on playgrounds in Kentucky, Tennessee, Kansas, and Nebraska. It is enjoyed by a wide age range of children.

Two children volunteer to be Hiram and Mirandy. One of them is blindfolded and led to the center of a circle of children, who are holding one another's hands. The object of the game is for the blindfolded one to find the elusive partner by calling out the name and groping toward the answering voice.

If Hiram is blindfolded, he calls out, "Mirandy?" Mirandy must answer each time, "Here, Hiram," as she moves quietly from where she was standing. The game is over when the calling partner touches the other one. Hiram and Mirandy choose two players to take their places and those players decide which will be blindfolded.

Texas Grunt ▲ ■

Players: at least 12 and a leader
Equipment: paper bags or scarves for blindfolds

This playground game is popular with children who know one another well.

One person volunteers to be It and is blindfolded. All other players form a circle with It in the center. To begin, the leader guides It around the circle, stopping in front of a player. The player grunts but says no words. It can say, "Grunt again." It can guess three times what the name of the player is. If a guess is correct, the grunter becomes It. If the three guesses are incorrect, It is guided to another person. The leader always goes in one direction and never stops at the same person twice. Older boys and girls are able to keep track of their guesses and the laughter that sometimes erupts from sections of the circle. Younger children are more likely to guess wildly and find the action humorous.

Duck, Duck, Goose

Players: 12 or more, ages 5 to 7

This playground game is easy for young children to teach newcomers.

One person volunteers to be It. Everyone else sits in a circle. To begin, It walks around the circle touching each person on the head and saying "Duck." After saying "Duck" several times, It says "Goose" instead and darts off. The player who is tapped at that point must stand up and try to catch It before It runs around the circle to the player's space. If It succeeds in sitting down safely, the running player is the new It. If the player catches It, It must start a new round of touching heads.

The Churches
Las Iglesias

Players: any even number over 6, ages 9 to 12
Equipment: a softball and bat

This is an old game in New Mexico and may have come from ancient Spain, where endangered persons were permitted sanctuary in the churches. In New Mexico it was played originally by the men of one village against those of another. Today older boys and girls can play in two teams of equal number.

The game is played on a large flat field with a softball and bat. At one end of the field is a rectangle or circle large enough for one whole team to stand in while it is at bat. This space is called the Big Church. The team at bat is called the inside team. About 40 or 50 feet from the Big Church is the Little Church, the space to which batters run when they hit a pitched ball. The pitcher on the other team stands about the same distance from the batter as the Little Church is from the Big Church. The members of the other team are fielders. The action is fast and goes like this:

Batters get only one strike but may wait for what they consider a good pitch. If a ball is caught in the air, the inside team is out and the other team becomes the inside team. If the ball rolls or goes over the fielders' heads, the batter runs to the Little Church and tries to run back to the Big Church before being touched with the ball. A batter may stay in the Little Church until another batter has a hit and it is safe to run back to the Big Church. If the ball is retrieved, team members may work together to tag, or "burn," the running batter. The runner may intercept a ball as it goes from fielder to fielder, reversing the decision to retire the side as inside team.

The position of a team may change several times in two or three minutes. Some well-matched teams manage to play long enough so that everyone bats. A weak team against a strong one may be "inside" for less than a minute before the other team prevails. When everyone on the inside team has been at bat and there are players in the Little Church waiting to be batted in, the inside team is out, no matter how successful it has been. The general practice is not to keep score. Winning is determined not by the number of hits but by the length of time spent as the inside team.

Do as I Do

Players: 6 to 12, ages 5 to 8, and a leader

This is a game found in some Latin American countries and played in the southwestern United States. A faster-paced version was played by young people and adults as a parlor game in the United States in the early 20th century.

To begin, everyone stands in a circle. The leader, who may be an older child or an adult, starts the game by saying, "Do as I do," and begins acting out a daily task. In a Hispanic home it might be making tortillas or serving tacos along with such ordinary tasks in any household as washing hands, combing hair, setting the table, sweeping, and so on. The leader continues the motion as all others in the circle copy it. When the leader changes action, the other players are to shift also without any noise. Those players who continue the old motion because they are not paying attention are fined. The leader says, "Sit down while *(name)* and *(name)* pay their penalties." Penalties are usually physical feats such as hopping 10 steps inside the circle, touching one's toes with one's fingers without bending the knees, or walking in a circle with a bag over one's head. After the penalties are performed the leader chooses another person to be leader.

Car Games ▲ ■

Recreational Vehicles vs. Tractor Trailers. This car game for two teams (if all passengers want to play) or for two persons is adapted from a very old game by a family who drove on interstate highways from the Pacific to the Atlantic Ocean. One team gets one point for each recreational vehicle (RV) the players spot. The other team earns a point for every truck with more than four wheels. A moving van doubles the score for the first team to spot it. The RV team loses its entire score if a tour bus overtakes and passes the car. The truck team loses its score if a tour bus approaches in on-coming traffic. The game is over when the car enters a rest stop.

This game can be played by two people on a city street with two-way traffic by counting red versus white cars. A delivery truck doubles the score for the first one to see it. The player counting red loses the entire score when a car with an out-of-state license plate is parked on the left. The other player loses when such a car is parked on the right.

I Spy. This is another car game for long-distance travel. An adult or older child makes a list of five things for the players, divided into two teams, to look for along the highway. They may be route numbers, state patrol cars, church steeples, bodies of water, lights or skyline of a city, or vehicles exactly like the one the players are in. Each time the players find an item they shout "I spy!" The team that finds all five of the items first wins the game.

On country roads with two-way traffic one team can spy items on the right and the other items on the left. The list might include a strip of stores, sheep or goats, fast food restaurants, silos or grain elevators, pedestrians, dogs without a leash, and so on.

Reading License Plates. This is a license plate game that is most fun played by everyone together for a brief time. The passengers read the license plates of passing vehicles and look for consecutive numbers 1 to 10, taking only one digit from a plate. For example, to begin, someone finds a 1. If there is a 2 on the same plate it does not count. It must be somewhere on another plate. The 10 is the hardest to find because the 1 and the 0 must be next to each other on the same plate.

States Game. This is an old question-and-answer game about states for 2 to 10 people that a family revived on an automobile trip. It had been a singing game, but the 8- and 10-year-old boys changed it to what they called rap (saying the words to a rhythm but no tune). The 5-year-old girl was highly amused at the "funny answers," but when she made up her own, it was evident that her enjoyment did not arise from the word plays of her older brothers. To play, one person asks the question and as many as know the answer reply. Here are the ones the family remembers.

Q. What did Delaware? Oh, what did Delaware?
A. She wore her New Jersey. Oh, she wore her New Jersey.

Q. Where is Indiana? Oh, where is Indiana?
A. Idaho, Alaska. Oh, Idaho Alaska.

Q. How did Wis-con-SIN? Oh, how did Wis-con-SIN?
A. He stole a Ken-tuc-KY. Oh, he stole a Ken-tuc-KY.

Q. How did Flori-DIE? Oh, how did Flori-DIE?
A. She died of MIZ-ouri. She died of MIZ-ouri.

Q. How did Cali-FONE? How did Cali-FONE?
A. She used her Caroline. Oh, she used her Caroline.

Q. What did Missis-SIP? Oh, what did Missis-SIP?
A. She sipped her Minnesota. Oh, she sipped her Minnesota.

Q. Where has O-re-GONE? Oh, where has O-re-GONE?
A. She's in the Arizone. Oh, she's in the Arizone.

Q. What did I-o-WAY? Oh, what did I-o-WAY?
A. She weighed a Washing-TON. Oh, she weighed a Washing-TON.

Q. What did O-hi-o? Oh, what did O-hi-o?
A. He owed his income Texas. Oh, he owed his income Texas.

Q. What did Ida-HO? Oh, what did Ida-HO?
A. She hoed a Mary-LAND. Oh, she hoed a Mary-LAND.

America
South of the Rio Grande

This region of South America, Central America, Mexico, and the Caribbean is enormous and includes many cultures—Indian, Spanish, Portuguese, African, and German to name only a few. Vast differences exist between the lives of the many children of poverty and those of the few children of considerable wealth. The persons reporting on Latin American games for this book chiefly described organized games in which an adult leader was present. The only exception was the observer at the border between United States and Mexico, where boys and girls meeting for the first time share their game lore, negotiate procedures, and adapt rules to their circumstances.

Some of the games in this section are similar to European games but are given a Latin American slant. Who Is It? and the Hawk and the Chickens are examples. Other games are clearly for parties, such as the Piñata game. Boys and girls in impoverished rural areas and poor urban neighborhoods are sometimes too busy eking out an existence to play games like those in this book. There are millions of street children in the cities of Brazil, some with homes in the *favelas* (slums) such as those at the very top of Rio de Janeiro and more with no homes at all. They do not play; they work in order to survive. The fortunate ones wash cars, shine shoes, and beg. More of them run "drug errands" or sell their bodies.

A man old enough to be their grandfather talked with a nine-year-old boy and his five-year-old sister:

"It's all luck," the boy explained. "Bad luck for me, good luck for them," and he pointed toward the high rises on the beach. "My sister here," he continued, "is still lucky. She doesn't know how to get money yet. That's lucky."

The number of impoverished, starving, exploited children is increasing all over the world, not just in Latin America and the so-called developing world. Luck is a serious, life-or-death issue, not a matter of hitting a piñata just right and getting a handful of candy. If we are to learn from history soon enough to prevent the near extinction of a generation of the world's people, concerned persons might look back at the rise of game playing among children released from the burden of work in the Western world's mills of the 19th century. Who were their advocates? What responsibility did lawmakers take? How were the churches and schools involved? How long did it take for loving kindness to win over injustice?

Winning and losing at games, in the best of all worlds, prepares the players for winning and losing as productive adults and cooperative neighbors. What happens to children who cannot afford to play?

Even or Odd
Pares o Nones

Equipment: an equal number (12 to 16) of small stones, acorns, or buttons for each player

No one knows by this time where the games played on the Mexican-United States border originally came from. Even or Odd is played on both sides.

One player distributes the playing pieces, which the players conceal behind a card or one hand. To begin, a player puts one, two, or three playing pieces in one hand and makes a fist. He or she holds out the hand to another player and asks, "Odd or even?" The guesser answers. If the guess is correct, the guesser wins all the pieces. If the answer is wrong, the guesser gives the asking player the same number of pieces as are in the hand. The game ends when a player is out of playing pieces or when the group decides to do something else. As players lose pieces it is important that other players not know how many pieces are left, making guessing and winning too easy.

Jumping Rope

Players: at least 4 who are adept at jumping rope
Equipment: 5 to 6 yards of 1/4-inch rope

Jumping rope is popular on the Rio Grande border between the United States and Mexico. Jumping by a group instead of an individual takes as many forms in this area as in Canada and the United States. For another jump roping game see Skipping Rope (page 169).

Teddy Bear. Rhymes chanted by the two rope twirlers and spectators are common. Here is one that is heard with variations from place to place. Jumpers act out the words.

> Teddy Bear, Teddy Bear, turn around;
> Teddy Bear, Teddy Bear, touch the ground;
> Teddy Bear, Teddy Bear, show your ragged shoe;
> Teddy Bear, Teddy Bear, better skiddoo.

On "skiddoo" the jumpers jump out and others jump in as the chant continues:

> Teddy Bear, Teddy Bear, go upstairs;
> Teddy Bear, Teddy Bear, say your prayers;
> Teddy Bear, Teddy Bear, turn out the light;
> Teddy Bear, Teddy Bear, say "Good night."

On "Good night" the jumpers jump out.

Clock. Another jumping game involving many players is called Clock. The object of the game is to mark each hour from 1 to 12 while two players twirl the rope for jumpers. To begin, the players line up waiting to jump. The first player enters, jumps

once, and runs out. The second one follows, jumps twice, and runs out. If there are fewer than 12 jumpers, the first players line up to continue the jumping until the last player jumps 12 times. Then the game begins again. When a jumper stumbles or is touched by the rope, he or she becomes a twirler and a twirler joins the jumpers. A child who cannot jump may serve as a permanent twirler.

Piñata ▲ ■

Players: no more than 12 to 15 of any age and 2 leaders
Equipment: 1 homemade piñata for 12 or 15 children, filled
  with wrapped candies and nuts in their shells; paper bag
  blindfolds; and a broomstick or cane

In Mexico a piñata game is played around Christmas and is largely for children. It has become known in many parts of the world as far from Mexico as India, for example, and it is no longer for children alone. The piñata is a container filled with candy and nuts suspended on a cord or rope at a height that children with sticks can reach in order to break it open. Piñatas are commonly made of papier maché painted and decorated with crepe paper.

Here is one way for a leader or other adult to make a piñata. Blow up a balloon about 18 inches long and 12 inches across at the widest place. Tie the mouthpiece and cover the

balloon with an even layer of ready-to-mix papier maché with the mouthpiece sticking out. Let dry in a warm, airy place. Deflate the balloon and remove it from the papier maché casing if possible. Paint the piñata in bright colors. Cut a hole in the back or top and put candy and nuts inside. Glue a piece of cardboard over the hole and cover it with more papier maché. Let it dry thoroughly. Cover with crepe paper streamers. Attach a screweye to the back of the piñata and fasten one end of a cord to it. The other end can be held by an adult leader when the children begin to play with it. Until then let it hang high up near the ceiling for all to see but not to touch.

One leader blindfolds the children as they take turns trying to hit and break the piñata. He or she gives the child who is first the stick, turns the child around two or three times, and says, "Now!" What the children watching know is that the other leader, who controls the other end of the cord, has dangled the piñata close to the player but out of reach of the stick. Those children who wish to challenge the first one may seek a turn. Before interest wanes, the piñata is lowered and children volunteer to break it. When the nuts and sweets finally crash to the floor, they are shared by everyone.

Three Taps
Los Tres Toquecitos

Players: at least 6, ages 8 to 12

This is a Hide-and-Seek game similar to Kick the Can in the United Kingdom (see page 98), but the players assume roles and carry on a dialogue. This dramatization is characteristic of Mexican and indeed most Latin American children's games.

The porter is It and the door is the goal. All other players are to hide when the porter faces the door and counts aloud to 100. The porter calls out, "Here I come, ready or not!" As the porter hunts, the players try to edge up to the door without being caught, knock three times, and shout, "One, two, three for me!" The first player to do this becomes the porter's helper, who can catch sight of another player, tag him or her, and shout, "One, two, three for *(name)*." Sometimes the player can outrun the porter or assistant to the door, knock three times, and shout, "One, two, three for me!" In some places the first player to be caught by the porter is the next porter. In other places the last player to be caught is the porter. The group playing Three Taps for the first time may decide which way to play the game.

The Hawk and the Chickens

Players: 9 to 12, ages 5 to 8

This game has been played differently over the years, but it is essentially a chasing game in which the mother hen protects the chickens from the hawk. This type of game is common in many areas. See, for example Eagle and Chickens from China (page 41). For a song about a hawk and chickens, see "Sansa Kroma" in *A World of Children's Songs*.

In this game the mother hen leads her brood in one line. The hawk is after only the last chick in line. The object of the game for the mother hen and other chicks is to protect the last chick. The object for the hawk is to get that last chick. The hawk is not after any of the others.

To begin, the hawk does not move. The mother hen and chicks walk past the hawk watching constantly. The mother hen tells the chicks, "Stay close. Hang on to the one in front of you. Tell me what the hawk is doing. We must protect our last chick." The chicks answer as the hawk moves, "He's moving, smiling, sharpening his beak; he's coming closer, closer, closer . . ." The mother hen can use her arms to keep the hawk away. The chicks, in a chain, try to protect the last chick by winding in a coil. The hawk cannot touch the other chicks but can swoop to the shoulders of the last chick.

Once caught, the last chick becomes the hawk for the next game, the hawk becomes the mother hen, and the former mother hen stands behind the new mother hen. The next-to-the-last chick becomes the new last chick. In three or four games, players have an opportunity to be the mother hen, hawk, last chick, or protective chicks.

Onions for Mamma

Players: at least 6, ages 8 to 12

Many games played by children in Puerto Rico are similar to those played by urban children in the United States and Canada. This one becomes the occasion for clowning while at the same time it is an opportunity to display muscular strength and running ability.

The group chooses one player to be the onion seller and another to be It. The other players are the onions. The onion seller stands with both hands clinging to the goal, usually a pole or tree. The onions stand in a line behind the onion seller with their arms around the waist of the player immediately in front.

It approaches the onion seller and says, "I need an onion for Mamma's soup."

"What happened to the one I sold you yesterday?" the onion seller asks.

"The rats ate it," It answers.

"Well, then," the onion seller says, "pick another one." It touches each onion on the top of the head with an index finger and says, "No good, soft, rotten . . ." until he or she comes to the last onion. "Hah! Just right for Mamma's soup!"

It tries to pull the last onion from the others while the onion hangs on with as much strength as possible. If It is not successful, he or she becomes the first onion, and the last onion is It. Generally, It is successful and takes the last onion to Its side and returns to the onion seller to request another onion. When all the onions are on Its side, they become dogs.

It then says to the onion seller, "Please come to eat soup with Mamma and me."

"Not I," says the onion seller. "You have too many dogs."

"Don't worry about the dogs," It tells the onion seller. "I will remove their teeth." It goes to the other players and claps in front of each face.

"Please come," It says to the onion seller. As the guest comes near, the dogs begin to bark. The onion seller runs toward the goal with the dogs in pursuit. If the onion seller reaches the goal without being caught, he or she becomes It for the next game and It becomes the first onion. All the dogs are turned back into onions. If the onion seller is caught before reaching the goal, a new game begins with the same onion seller. The dog who tagged the onion seller in the last game becomes It.

Disconnect

Players: 8, ages 5 and above, and a leader

This team game of chasers and chased is played in many other countries under many other names. It has some similarity to Kick the Can as it is played in Scotland and Relievo as played in northern England (see pages 98 and 97).

The players form two teams by complete chance, the youngest player acting as blind chooser. The chooser rests on hands and knees with head down and eyes closed. The leader taps the chooser's head three times and says, "One, two, three, chaser or chased?" pointing to one player. The chooser answers and the leader shows the player where to stand. The leader must see that the sides are even in number and may say, "One more chaser and one more chased," to let the chooser know how the sides are balanced. The object of the game is for the chasers to bring the chased to base, an area big enough for the whole team to stand. The chased, however, try to stay away from the chasers and to rescue their fellow team members from the base.

To begin, the leader shouts, "One!" and the chased begin to run. The leader continues, "Two! Three!" with which the chasers set out after the other team. When a chaser catches one player, the captor must touch the captive on the back three times while shouting, "One, two, three—connect!" The captive tries to keep the chaser from doing so and may succeed in escaping. Once a chaser takes a player to the base, another of the chased team may run to the base, touch the team member on the back three times, and call out, "One, two, three—disconnect!" Then the player is free to run again.

Because the sides are chosen by chance there is no predictable way for the game to end. When all chased players are at the base the game is over. Or when chasers keep losing quarry from the base, players may decide to start a second game by switching sides. When the game is played by 8 to 10 older children it can become very competitive. When played by a wide age range of children, the older tend to rescue the younger and prolong the game.

Martinillo

Players: at least 10, ages 5 to 7
Equipment: a cloth belt

This is one of the many Latin American games with conversation between It and another player, in this case, Martinillo (mar-tee-NEE-yo).

Two players are chosen to be It and Martinillo. All other players stand in the circle with a space for Martinillo. It chases Martinillo around the circle trying to hit him with a cloth belt. Here is their dialogue as they run:

It: Martinillo!
Martinillo: Si, señor (or señorita).
It: Where is your burro?
Martinillo: I sold it.
It: Where is your money?
Martinillo: I gambled it away.
It: Where are your dice?
Martinillo: I burned them.
It: Where are the ashes?
Martinillo: On your shirt.
It: Where is the salt?
Martinillo: In its proper place.

At this point both It and Martinillo try to get to the place in the circle reserved for Martinillo. If Martinillo gets there first, another player is chosen to run. If It gets there first, Martinillo gets the belt and is It, and another player is Martinillo.

Ring on a String

Players: at least 10, ages 5 and above, and a leader
Equipment: a ring and a ball of string

This game, which requires sharp eyes and skillful fingers, has variations in many parts of the world.

The object of the game is for It to spot a ring traveling on a circular string held by many players. The players sit close together in a circle. One of the older players stands inside the circle as It. The players pass a string all around the circle; the leader slips a ring on it and ties the string in a knot that the ring can slip over easily. The players take hold of the string with both hands in loose fists so that the ring can pass from one to another without It noticing. As the ring moves, all the players keep moving their own hands from where they are touching each other to where each hand is touching a neighbor's. It is quite possible that most players do not know where the ring is until it reaches one of their hands. They learn to pretend they have the ring to try to confuse It. Skillful players can send the ring in the opposite direction when they think It is about to guess its whereabouts.

When It finds the ring, the player who has it becomes It and It sits where the player sat. If It guesses incorrectly three times, the leader says to It, "Shut your eyes, turn to the north, south, east, and west. Now point to the one to take your place." The game goes on with a new It.

In a variation of this game played by older children in the United States and Canada, players sit in a row or circle without a string but with fists close together as they pass a stone from one hand to another. Each player pretends to have the stone and to pass it on while It tries to detect who really has it.

Trapping the Sun

Players: 10 to 15, ages 5 to 8, or 7 players, ages 9 to 12

Traditionally in Peru, ever since Inca times, the sun was regarded as an elusive supreme being. In this game, children try to trap the sun. The game can be fast and rough, demanding skill on every player's part.

Two children are chosen to be the sun and It. The others form a semicircle. Their objective is to trap the sun and let It go.

To begin, It chases the sun somewhere outside the semicircle. The players join hands waiting for It to pull the sun into the semicircle. The sun tries to run from the other players. When the sun comes near one end or the other of the semicircle, the players and It, working together, never separately, try to close in on the sun, leaving It on the outside. Children with experience being the sun are occasionally hard to trap.

Older children play the game with fewer trappers. They do not join hands until the capture is certain.

Swing and Seek

Players: 4 to 8, ages 5 to 7

This game is believed to have begun in the Ecuadorean countryside when hammocks were tied in between trees. Today it is played in city parks where children push one another in swings and have places they can hide.

The players divide into two groups, which need not be the same size. One group sits in the swings, and the other group pushes the swingers until they are high in the air. Then those who were pushing run off to hide all in one place while the swings come slowly to a halt. This action is called letting "the old cat die down." All the swingers go together to hunt for the hiders. When the swingers find them the swingers chase them and try to tag them before they can get back to the swings and sit in them. If half or more of the hiders are tagged, they become swingers and the first swingers push them in a second game.

Some children play the game with a single swinger and hiders who run off to individual spots. When the old cat dies down, the swinger shouts, "Ready or not, here I come." Any hider can come into safety by sitting in the swing while the swinger is looking for hiders. When other hiders come in, they must touch the person in the swing to be safe themselves. When the hunter finds a hider, the hunter tries to get back to the swing first and says, "One, two, three for *(name)*." The last person to be caught in such a manner is the swinger for the next game.

Mail Delivery

Players: competent swimmers of any age and 3 judges, teenage or adult

Equipment: materials for making paper boxes and strings for each player

This game of skill is played by expert swimmers along the Amazon River. It is a swimming race for players who like to swim on their backs.

The players make paper boxes according to the following directions. Collect $8^1/2$ x 11-inch sheets of paper, a ruler, scissors, white glue, and a ball of kitchen string. Fold the paper on the dotted lines as shown in the diagram. Cut the paper on the solid lines. Glue side A to side E. Fold the ends together to make sturdy sides on the box and glue them securely. Tie a string around the box as if for mailing it, keeping the ends long enough to tie around the swimmer's head. The judges tie a box on each swimmer's head so that it rests on the forehead.

The object of the game is to swim a short distance without getting the package on the forehead wet. The goal is not speed but the condition of the package upon delivery. Players need not all begin at the same time, but the packages should be judged within moments of arrival.

Cho-cho-chuckie

Players: 10 to 15, ages 5 to 8
Equipment: ball made of a rolled-up pair of heavy socks

This is a game played by Brazilian children whose parents work on farms. Some of the researchers of games believe it came to Brazil from Africa. "Cho-cho-chuckie" is what a Brazilian child calling chickens seems to say when the sounds are rendered into English.

One person is It. Everyone else sits in a circle. It skips around the outside of the circle saying, "Cho-cho-chuckie, cho-cho-chuckie." Very quietly and quickly It drops the sock ball behind a player, who gets up, picks up the ball, and runs after It, trying to tag It before It arrives at the runner's place. It usually arrives first and must stand on one foot, holding the other foot with one hand. The rule is that one can change the leg one is standing on but must continue to stand on one foot or the other until almost the end of the game.

The new It proceeds to run around those seated in the circle and drop the ball behind another player, repeating what happened before. When every player except the last one to be It is standing on one foot, It shouts, "It's raining!" Players scatter, running on both feet, until It finally tags one and says, "You're It" for another game.

Sick Cat
Gato Doente

Players: at least 6, ages 5 to 9

Variations of this game are played in many parts of the world. It is most fun for the players when running and chasing skills are about the same.

One person is chosen to be Gato ("Cat"). Gato begins the game by shouting, "One, two, three! Here I come!" All other players run away from Gato. Gato can tag them on their head, shoulders, elbows, or knees. When they are tagged, players become sick cats and must keep one palm on the place Gato touched them as they chase other players for Gato. Their job is to corner or hold a player while crying, "Gato! Gato!" until the chief cat comes to tag the player. The one who escapes being captured by either Gato or one of the other sick cats becomes Gato for the next game.

Children on the border between Mexico and the United States on the Rio Grande play a version of this game that they call Spot Tag. When a player is tagged, he or she becomes It and must hold one hand on the tagged spot while chasing other players. After another player is tagged and is It, former tagged players continue to hold on to the tagged spots as they run from It.

The Chief Commands ▲
Chef Mande

Players: 2 to 10, ages 5 to 7

A child can play this game while visiting someone who is confined to a bed. It is similar to Simon Says.

The person who is It says, "The Chief commands you to point to something blue." All other players point to something blue. If It says only, "Point to something blue," without saying, "The Chief commands . . . ," the players are to do nothing. It soon learns to give three or four commands in rapid succession with the last one having no orders from the Chief.

There are several ways to become It. If two people are playing, each time a mistake is made the player and It change jobs. When there are more players, the first player to make five mistakes become It. The game in which the person who makes a mistake is out of the game is very unpopular with most children, and they will negotiate another ending if permitted to do so.

Chicken Fight
Luta de Galho

Players: 2, ages 9 to 12
Equipment: 2 head scarves or neckerchiefs

This is a game of skill between two players, usually girls in Brazil, but boys can play too. The winner may challenge someone else. Good players attract a cheering group of spectators of all ages.

Each of the players tucks a head scarf or neckerchief into the belt or waistband. The object of the game is to gain possession of the opponent's scarf, but the obstacles are challenging.

To begin, the players face each other, stand on one foot, and keep one arm folded across the chest. With the other arm each player tries to pluck the scarf from the other's waist, all the time hopping on one foot. A player protects her or his scarf by nudging the opponent with the elbow of the folded arm, but it is against the rules to extend that arm.

Beginning players are allowed four fouls each before losing to the opponent without the capture of a scarf. Fouls include putting both feet on the ground at one time or extending the folded arm. The winner is the one who snatches the other's scarf or the one with the fewer foul plays. In challenge games the players negotiate the number of fouls, always less than four. A player may always choose which leg to hop on and which arm to fold. Some left-sided aces are quite inept hopping and nudging on the right side.

Who Is It?
¿Quién Es?

Players: 10 to 15, ages 8 to 12, and a leader

This game helps newcomers learn names and faces while the players who are already well acquainted take their turns at being It. The game can be played inside or out of doors.

Players form a line with It at the head. They speak their names in turn. Then It takes nine steps forward while all other players change places in line. A leader or someone appointed by the group puts a large paper bag over Its head. It must guess who is immediately behind him or her without touching or conversing with that player. "Who is it" ("¿Quién es?") the players ask all together. It gets one guess to begin with and then may ask three questions. Experienced players learn to narrow the possibilities: Is it a boy or girl? Does her first name start with A to M or N to Z in the alphabet? Is she taller or shorter than (name)? Then It must guess the name of the player in order to get another turn at the head of the line. If It misses, another player is It.

Fish

Players: 12 or more, ages 8 to 12

This is a game to play at the beach. It is somewhat like Fruit Basket Upset but is based on a game played by younger children in Chile. It moves fast and is full of surprises. It makes a welcome change between eating lunch and listening to a story.

To begin, players stand in a large circle with It somewhere inside. The object for It is to get a place to sit in the circle. It whispers the name of a fish to each player: bass, tuna, whiting, turbot, flounder, marlin, for example. It may give everyone a different fish name or the same one to several people. Then they sit on the ground. Any neighboring players may exchange fish names so that It is never sure who has what name.

To begin the action It says, "Bass and tuna, find new places." If only two players have those names, they exchange

places while It tries to scamper to the place where one was sitting. The challenge to the players is in not knowing how many bass and tuna there are in the circle and where to run before It finds a place. If It decides to give only four or five fish names and calls all others flounder, the players may be surprised as It says:

"Trout and sole, find new places."
"Haddock and halibut, find new places."
"Haddock and flounder find new places."

Almost always It gets a place when the players are surprised. The person without a place in the circle becomes It. The new It may say, "All flounder become your choice of trout, haddock, or halibut." Or It may give everyone a new fish name. When It has become unsuccessful in getting a place in the circle, he or she may call, "Shark!" at which time all players scurry to shift and It easily finds a place.

Oceania

Many of the games played in Oceania (Pacific islands, New Zealand, Australia, the Malay Archipelago, and the Philippines) came originally from European countries that once dominated the Pacific. They have taken on local characteristics but are still recognizable as Soccer, Hide and Seek, and Tag. Other games were invented by native peoples. In New Zealand the Maoris' games have become popular within the whole society. Although some of them bear a similarity to games European children played 200 years ago, the Maori hand, stick, and string games had utilitarian purposes. They prepared children for the warfare, hunting, and weaving they would do as adults.

The mystery of the origin of the string games of the Pacific (*whai*) will probably never be solved. They pre-date the coming of the Europeans, and family stories reveal their popularity with young and old. In fact, the most efficient way to learn *whai* is not from intricate diagrams but from a teacher. What has stumped ethnologists is the appearance of exactly the same intricate string games among North American Indians, Arctic Inuit, and Pacific islanders. Allan and Paulette Macfarlan explain and illustrate these games in *Handbook of American Indian Games* (1985). The Maori myth about string games, according to Allen Armstrong in *Maori Games and Hakas* (1964), is that Maui, the Maoris' ancient hero, brought Cat's Cradle to his people. Some of the complicated designs were executed by three players and depicted legends of the people. In modern times *whai* have been taught to students of piano and embroidery, and in at least one instance *whai* were used as treatment of some disabled war veterans who were regaining the use of their fingers.

Another mystery is the origin of the yo-yo. Many countries claim it, from China to Greece, but the most recent persuasive arguments favor the Philippines. It is possible that yo-yos and Cat's Cradle have arisen in more than one culture as products of the human mind and talent. It is also enticing to consider a people older than recorded history in the days before New Zealand floated away from Asia and there was no Bering Strait between North America and Asia. Perhaps a grandmother taught a young child to make a cat's cradle while a grandfather carved a yo-yo for the very first time.

Elephant, Man, and Ant ▲

Players: 2, ages 5 to 12

This game is played by two people to see whose turn is first. It is similar to Paper, Scissors, Stone from China and Japan (see page 43).

The players face each other with right hands behind their heads. They count aloud, "One, two, three, go!" On the word "go" they hold out their right hands in one of three ways: the thumb, index finger, or little finger is pointed toward the opposite player.

> The pointed thumb is the elephant.
> The pointed index finger is the man.
> The pointed little finger is the ant.

To decide who is winner the players say whichever of the following lines is appropriate to their two gestures:

> "Elephant wins over man because he can trample on him."
> "Man wins over ant because he can step on him."
> "Ant wins over elephant because he can run up his trunk and tickle him to death."

If the players make the same sign, they play the game again.

Kinder Kaatsen

Players: 4 to 6, ages 8 to 12
Equipment: bats and a softball, or a volleyball

Before 1949 Indonesia was a territory of the Netherlands, and many Dutch families went to live there. They took with them this Dutch game, simplified for their own children, and it became popular with the Indonesian children as well. It is good exercise for active children.

The playing area is divided in two by drawing a chalk line or using a painted line already on the floor. The players form two equal teams and choose which side each team will take. Some children play with a bat and ball, but the game is more fun with a volleyball and the players' hands as bats.

To begin, one player serves the ball to the opposite side. A player on that side who is nearest the ball may bat it back while it is in the air or after it bounces once. The object is to keep the ball in play as long as possible. There is no foul line and no scoring, but players on the same side must stay in their part of the court and not interfere with another player's attempt to bat the ball.

Cock Fight

Players: 12, ages 5 to 8

In this game the children imitate chickens. It is a form of Squat Tag (see page 115) except that all players squat with hands under their knees.

To begin, one person marks off on the playground a rectangular area in which the squatting chickens can move around, still squatting. The object of the game is for It (the cock), who is also squatting, to pursue and touch one of the players with his or her head without Its losing balance. A skillful It learns how to corner a squatter at the edge of the playing area and to tag someone who is losing his or her balance.

Touch Pole Tag

Players: at least 6, ages 5 to 8

Variations of this game are played on several large islands in the Philippines.

Players form a big ring around the touch pole (a flag pole or a tree) with plenty of space between players. It stands at the touch pole and commands the players to move in certain ways: "Walk," "Hop," "Jump." When It says, "Run!" the game of tag begins. It tries to catch the players before they can touch the pole and be safe temporarily. Those who are caught are out of the game. Pole touchers can stay at the pole only until It chases another player. The last person left to be tagged is It for the next game.

Yo-yo

Players: 1 or more
Equipment: a yo-yo for each player

Many countries claim the yo-yo, but the name comes from the Philippines. It is an enjoyable game that young children can learn from older ones.

First the older child shows the younger how to wind up the yo-yo and put an index finger through the loop at the end of the string. Then the experienced player works the yo-yo up and down and coaches the beginner. It is important for the two to practice long enough so that the beginner sees signs of improvement. Children learn quickly from others and emulate the champions even to teaching others in their turn.

Boiri

Players: at least 4, of the same size
Equipment: a ball made of a pair of heavy socks

This game was originally played with a ball woven of coconut leaves. It resembles Soccer without the structure. Younger children play it without scoring.

The object of the game is to keep the ball in the air at all times without using the hands at all. The players can kick it, hit it with their heads, and bounce it off their shoulders or thighs. Older boys and girls divide into teams. The two team captains flip a coin to decide which player will kick the ball into the air to begin the game. When the ball is lost, the player who finds it must not pick it up with the hands but point to it with the nose.

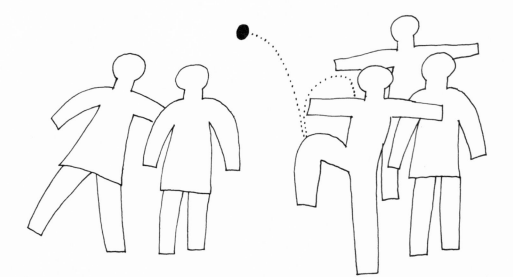

Follow the Leader

Players: at least 6, the more the better; ages 5 to 12

This time-tested outdoor sport is played in New Zealand and in many other countries as well.

A leader is chosen by the group, generally a person with a reputation of finding a wide variety of ways to act. The players line up behind the leader with enough space between to swing their arms and legs without hitting a neighbor. The leader strides, hops, turns somersaults, twirls about, and crawls as the followers imitate each action. In rural areas the leader often looks for difficult feats—leaping over ditches, walking through wooded areas, climbing hills, and skipping through bogs. It is the leader's job to keep the followers active. If they are displeased or bored with what they are expected to do, they can stop and as a group discuss their disapproval with the leader. If they are tired, they can request a rest. The game usually comes to an end without incident and the group takes up another pastime.

An urban version of the game is a sidewalk hike in which children do as the leader does for a specified distance. At a corner the child at the end of the line comes forward to be the new leader and flips a coin to decide in what direction to go. The child states which side of the coin is "right" and which "left." The former leader takes a place immediately behind the new leader.

Walking on Stilts

Players: any number but only 1 person at a time to a pair of
stilts
Equipment: 1 or more pairs of stilts

Adults in many countries have used stilts as a way of moving
around on marshy ground. A 16th-century Dutch painting of
children's games shows a boy on stilts. Farmers and shep-
herds still walk on stilts.

Maori children probably learned about stilts from British
settlers in New Zealand. They walk on stilts and even race on
them.

Children vary in the speed with which they learn to balance and then walk on stilts. Beginners need a pair with footrests no more than six to eight inches from the ground. The
more skilled walkers can give hints to the learners and as they
improve can lend them stilts with higher footrests.

Skipping Rope

Players: 6 to 8, ages 7 to 10
Equipment: 6 yards of rope 1/4 inch in diameter

Children in many countries skip rope individually. In times past older Maori teenagers were adept at skipping rope in a group. Today children do it. For another skipping rope game see Jumping Rope (page 136).

Two people twirl the rope over the players' heads and under their feet as the players run in one by one and jump over the moving rope. They continue to run in and jump until there is no more room.

Another form of the game is for the two people holding the rope to rock it back and forth rather than to twirl it over the players' heads. With each successive game the rocking rope is held higher and higher from the ground until only champions can jump over it. Beginning jumpers need much practice by themselves before engaging in group efforts.

Geckos and Beetles

Players: at least 8, ages 5 to 12
Equipment: 2 wooden blocks each for gecko

This game of Tag is played at night in the Northern Territory of Australia, where the gecko, a nocturnal lizard, looks for beetles to eat.

The younger children are the beetles, who stand anywhere on the field. The older children are geckos and must each carry two wooden blocks. They clap the blocks together five times and shout, "Here we come, ready or not." They also clap whenever they tag a beetle. Clapping cuts down on the geckos' speed somewhat and makes the game a fair one. When geckos touch beetles, the beetles sit down together and wait until all are caught.

Playing Possum

Players: at least 6, ages 8 to 12

This game of Hide and Seek from the Australian outback is played by moonlight, traditionally by boys, although girls can play in the West.

Players divide into hunters and flying possums. The hunters sit with their head between their knees and count aloud to 100 while the flying possums hide. The possums also move about to elude the hunters. When a possum is caught, he or she accompanies a hunter but does not help the hunter. The game is over when all flying possums have been captured.

Conkers

Players: 2, ages 8 to 12
Equipment: horse chestnuts, 24-inch cord, and a long poultry
skewer

Conkers is a game played with a frenzy each autumn when horse chestnuts are in season. (A conker is a horse chestnut on a cord.) For many years it was considered a boy's game, but girls have become ardent players as well.

Conkers games are played in the United Kingdom (British settlers took the game to Australia) and the midwestern United States with essentially the same rules. The language used by the players varies from locality to locality.

The object of the game is for each opponent to strike the other one's conker and crack and break it with his or her own conker. The fun of the game begins with throwing stones at the finest horse chestnuts, which, school-child lore has it, are the highest ones on the tree.

The preparation of the conker is next. Enthusiasts have their preferences: baking it for half an hour, soaking it in salt or soda water or vinegar, or simply putting it in a cupboard to shrivel and toughen for a year. Using a long poultry skewer, the player makes a hole through the chestnut without cracking the edges of the hole. Then he or she pulls a 24-inch cord or shoestring through the chestnut and makes a knot at the bottom big enough and tight enough so that the chestnut cannot slip off during the contest.

To play, each opponent wraps the cord around his or her hand twice and lets the conker dangle. The first player who shouts, "First blow!" has first chance to strike. The other person holds one arm out to the side with the conker hanging down about eight inches. The challenger has three chances to strike; he or she holds the cord of his or her conker between the thumb and index finger while casting at the other's conker. If the struck conker breaks, the striking conker becomes a "oner" and earns a reputation as it strikes and breaks other conkers, becoming a "sixer" or a "tener" according to its successes. If the striking conker hits but does not break the other conker, the challenged player becomes the challenger. If the cords become tangled, the first player to shout "Clinks!" gets another shot. If both conkers break on contact, there is no score.

Most of the time children handle their own conker games, but occasionally certain prideful challengers attract the attention of a whole playground of spectators. An adult leader can help the players by reminding them that their way of playing games will be imitated by a younger "generation."

Taws

Players: at least 2
Equipment: 10 marbles per player

Taws or tors are shooters (marbles shot from the hand) in Tasmania. There are many games to play with them. Beginners enjoy this one.

Each player contributes five marbles to make a pile of them on the ground. Then with a stick one person draws a circle about 12 inches across around the pile of marbles. The first player stands at the edge of the circle and throws a taw on the marbles. Any that roll out of the circle belong to that player. If the player misses, he or she must sacrifice a marble to the

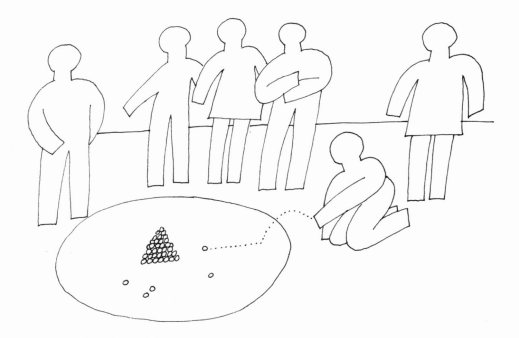

pile. The taw is still the player's property. Everyone has a turn until all the marbles are rolled out of the circle. Then they are returned to their original owners.

More-experienced players draw a circle about a yard across. They contribute three to five marbles depending upon the number playing. The marbles are spaced evenly in the circle. Each player has a taw. Boys and girls teach one another the secrets of shooting. In general, the thumb rests on the index finger just outside the ring. The taw is propelled by a flick of the thumb. Aim improves with practice. The object of the game is to shoot someone's marble out of the circle and possess it. The taw is always reclaimed after the turn. Players take turns, and the game is over when the circle is empty. Some skilled players like to play for "keeps." The less adept can lose a store of marbles quickly. An adult leader can call a meeting in order to negotiate rules of possession. In recent times the marbles more and more often return to the original owners after the game is over.

Bibliography

Amand, Mulk Raj. *Some Street Games of India*. New Delhi: National Book Trust, 1983.

Ariès, Philippe. *Centuries of Childhood: A Social History of Family Life*. New York: Random House, Vintage Books, 1962.

Armstrong, Alan. *Maori Games and Hakas*. Sydney: A.H. and A.W. Reed, 1964.

Arnold, Arnold. *The World Book of Children's Games*. New York: World Publishing Co., 1972.

Avedon, Elliot, and Brian Sutton-Smith. *The Study of Games*. Melbourn, Fla.: Robert E. Krieger Publishing Co., 1979.

Bancroft, J.H. *Games for the Playground, Home, School, and Gymnasium*. New York: Macmillan, 1909.

Bartlett, Vernon. *The Past of Pastimes*. Hamden, Conn.: Shoe String Press, Archon Books, 1969.

Bell, R.C. *Board and Table Games from Many Civilizations*. New York: Dover Publications, 1979.

Croke, Katherine, and Betty Fairchild. *Let's Play Games*. Chicago: National Easter Seal Society for Crippled Children and Adults, 1978.

Gruenfeld, Frederic V. *Games of the World: How to Make Them, How to Play Them, How They Came to Be*. Zurich: Swiss Committee for UNICEF, 1982.

Lazar, Wendy. *The Jewish Holiday Book*. New York: Doubleday and Co., 1977.

Macfarlan, Allan, and Paulette Macfarlan. *Games from Bible Lands and Times*. New York: Association Press, 1965.

_____. *Handbook of American Indian Games*. 1958. New York: Dover Publications, 1985.

Maguire, Jack. *Hopscotch, Hangman, Hot Potato, and HaHaHa: A Rulebook of Children's Games.* Englewood Cliffs, N.J.: Prentice Hall, 1990.

Millen, Nina. *Children's Games from Many Lands.* Rev. ed. New York: Friendship Press, 1965.

Opie, Iona, and Peter Opie. *Children's Games in Street and Playground.* New York: Oxford University Press, 1969.

_____. *The Lore and Language of School Children.* New York: Oxford University Press, 1987.

U.S. Bureau of Indian Affairs. *Social Plays, Games, Marches, Old Folk Dances, and Rhythmic Movements.* Washington, D.C.: U.S. Government Printing Office, 1911.

Vinton, Iris. *Folkways Omnibus of Children's Games.* Harrisburg, Pa.: Stackpole Books, 1970.

Wagenwoord, James. *Hangin' Out: City Kids, City Games.* New York: J.B. Lippincott, 1974.

Workers of the Writers' Program. *The Spanish-American Song and Game Book.* New York: A.S. Barnes and Co., 1942.

Index by Title

Index by Country